"In-Debt" to "Debt-Free:"

Life's Roadmap to Financial Security

by

Robert F. Newkirk, Jr.

Additional copies can be obtained from the publisher:

Jwahir
ENTERPRISES

www.jwamoney.com

First Edition

Manufactured in the United States of America.
Printed in China by Sunquest Printing.
http://www.sunquestprint.com

Library of Congress Control Number: 201310xxx
ISBN: 978-1-7368583-4-9

Contents

INTRODUCTION:
In-Debt to Debt-Free!

The world economy has shifted. It has shifted into a new paradigm, into a new era. Yet it seems that we haven't noticed. Oh, at first, it looked like the economy was taking its normal downturn as the bear market reigned supreme like it has done periodically over the past 60 years. The bear market came in 1987, and then it rebounded into a bull market that drove the Dow Jones Industrial Average from 2000 in the year 1992 to over 11,000 in the year 2000. So, the bear market appeared again in 2008, just like a repeated cycle. But something is different this time. An era has shifted, and we are not ready for it.

There is access to more customers on a global level than ever before with a whole lot less overhead. This era has the potential for everyone to make their own footprint. But we are not ready for it.

Why are we not ready for it? What is the difference in managing money now for the entrepreneur as the age of Social Media is starting to mature?
The internet has potentially put everyone on even ground, whereas in the past, the odds were stacked based on who owned more property to conduct business. There is access to more customers on a global level than ever before with a whole lot less

overhead. This era has the potential for everyone to make their own footprint. But we are not ready for it. Most people are not ready to take their possessions during this period, let alone sustain it. Why? We are still mentally stuck in the industrial revolution way of thinking and making money. If we don't shift with the new technology era and take action to change our status, people will be left further behind financially, and the effects will be more devastating than ever before. We have to put first things first. What do I mean by that? There is an order to this madness. We are not ready for it because we are out of order. Things that come first precede the things that will sustain them. It is like building a skyscraper. Before they can build the building up, they first must dig down. When the latest Smithsonian in Washington DC was erected, they had to dig deep down below the surface until they found stable ground to build the museum's foundation on. Once that was done, and the foundation was laid out, only then could they start to build up to its completion. The same is for building our financial foundation for this next era. The foundation is essential for success.

Here is an example. There is this restaurant that has employed on its staff three dishwashers. Each dishwasher earns a salary of $15,000 per year. So, the owner pays out $45,000 each year to keep his dishes cleaned and maintained. Suddenly, a new technology comes out consisting of a machine that is capable of cleaning and maintaining the equivalent of three dishwasher labor-hours of dishes. The cost of the machine is $20,000, with a maintenance fee of $5000 each year to keep the machine operational. So, the owner looks at the total costs of operating the machine versus keeping the three dishwashers employed. It becomes clear that by purchasing the machine and releasing the employed dishwashers, he would be saving $20,000 the first year and $40,000 each year afterward. So, he let go of the dishwashers. Their position as dishwashers has become OBE (overcome by events).

Although recent governmental statistics state that unemployment has decreased for the past couple of years, they have not really addressed the fact that the increased unemployment of 2008 has come back down with people making a lot less pay now in 2019.

However, the dishwashers do not realize that they need to rebrand themselves with another trade or skill. Instead, they proceed to print and circulate their resumes out into the job market, looking for another dishwashing position. They do not realize that every restaurant out there has discovered the fact that the new machine can wash their dishes faster, more efficiently, and cheaper. They do not realize that the dishwashing position they are applying for no longer exists. So why are they still circulating their resumes?

I am concerned about the dynamics of the economy for the last eight years and how they have left the state of true unemployment. Although until COVID came into play in 2020, recent governmental statistics stated that unemployment had decreased for the past couple of years. They have not really addressed the fact that the increased unemployment of 2008 has come back down with people making a lot less pay now in 2021. Inflation has increased over that time, and interest rates have had weird behaviors but are up slightly since that time. Until 2020, I believe that unemployment had decreased, but underemployment had doubled. The underemployment statistic, however, is not being kept by the government. Now with the addition of COVID-19, the underemployment is being further masked while unemployment jumps back into the headline. Promising increased job opportunities during a campaign is fine unless most of those jobs are hourly fast-food positions. The aerospace industry is under pressure to reduce the workforce by 10%, which represents better-paying jobs. There is also pressure for corporations to do more with fewer personnel. Until this trend is reversed, the underemployment rate will continue to increase.

Approximately 132 million individuals do not demonstrate the necessary savings skills and tools to survive another period of recession.

An epidemic is brewing for households growing accustomed and conforming to the financial crisis that has made its appearance since 2008. According to a new report conducted by the Corporation for

Enterprise Development, approximately 132 million individuals do not demonstrate the necessary savings skills and tools to survive another period of recession. Many are also ill-equipped to fund and sustain long-term financial goals such as healthcare, educational expenses, and residential housing. What has made it even worse is the habitual use of credit cards by holders in their late twenties and early thirties, who carry more debt than older consumers and make repayment at a far slower rate. In my opinion, paying credit card interest is the dumbest thing and the most destructive thing a person can do to their financial portfolio. Yet, so many people are doing just that without realizing it. The credit card bum rush starts the moment you graduate from high school. Prospective college students are pursued with supposedly "free money" from credit card companies requiring no credit history to receive your first $5,000 in credit. Students, having no peril as to what they have signed up for and who are desperate for some extra cash, use the credit card with no plan whatsoever to pay it back. Then suddenly, something called interest charges starts to accumulate at a whopping 22% rate. Yet, they have no idea what that will mean six months later when they still have not paid it off.

According to researchers, individuals born between 1985 and 1989 carry on an average of $5,970 more in debt than their parents had at their age and a staggering $9,267 more than their grandparents. I blame it in part on the reckless spending habits that the internet generation has acquired by handling a single keystroke in their own home without going out to see what it is they are buying. Even more so, I will point the finger to the problem of a fundamental lack of financial education that the recent generations have been exposed to. I had to think about that when I said it. When I was in high school, there were no classes that focused on financial education. As a matter of fact, if it weren't for my financial mentor when I was serving in the military forces, I still may not have been exposed to financial education.

In my opinion, paying credit card interest is the dumbest thing and the most destructive thing a person can do to their financial portfolio.

We were told to get an education (relatively speaking), get a good-paying job, and work hard to earn money. But nobody said anything about what to do once you receive it. How do you keep track of it? How do you set yourself up to keep it? Nobody ever made mention to me how slippery money is. Maybe it is because I never knew exactly what money meant and how its relationship with me should go. I had to find a way to seek that information out.

My personal experience of learning how slippery money came when I was in college. I went to school on an Air Force ROTC scholarship. We received a stipend of $100 per month as a part of it. I always looked forward to receiving that check. It served as a symbol of my educational accomplishments up until that point. One evening, I was preparing to go with some of my friends out to attend the college party of the week. I stopped by the ATM machine to pull out a $20 bill to take with me. When I got there and put in my bank card, all I got out was a message of non-sufficient funds. There was less than $10 in my account. So, I paused for a moment. I just deposited that stipend check into my account. Why is this machine telling me that I do not have any cash? I tried to recall what I could have spent that stipend on. All I could come up with was $25. Where did that other $65 go? From that point on, I had to come up with a system such that never again would I have to guess where my money went. And I had to know down to the penny. Pennies will eventually add up to dollars. I had to make sure that my money was able to work for me instead of losing money due to its slippery nature. Am I using money, or is money using me?

Money is nothing more than a piece of paper with a presidential figure on the front of it. However, the value of money is based on what we are motivated by and the means that we use to get it. Money has a tremendous impact on our freedom to live life to the fullest or spend most of our time making a living. So once again, I will ask the question, if money has the potential to be such a main focus in our lives, why are we not taught about it and how to manage and use it while growing up in secondary schools or even as a college course outside of accounting practices and macroeconomics?

Capitalism is most successful when 93% of the people that participate in it play the role of the consumer.

Well, in my previous book, THEE Diamond of Life: Redefining and Releasing Your Inner Gift of Power, I spoke on the uncanny relationship between economics and war and how that supported the present state of capitalism in the United States. The main emphasis is that capitalism is most successful when 93% of the people that participate in it play the role of the consumer. So, it would be counter-intuitive for a capitalist system to educate those same people about managing money. The perspective they need for us to have is to view money as a hot potato. As soon as we receive our paychecks, we must go out that weekend and make several consumer purchases using up every dime that we just earned. We are handing over our earnings to the remaining 7% who classify themselves as investors. Investors are the ones who make money in a capitalist system.

Isaiah 43:18-19 says, "Do not remember the former things, Nor consider the things of old. Behold, I will do a new thing, Now it shall spring forth;
Shall you not know it? I will even make a road in the wilderness And rivers in the desert."

My purpose for this book is to make you aware of the need to shift your consumer-prone habits and learn how to become investor-prone and money conscious. You can execute the transition and enjoy the financial freedom that the 10% enjoy without working yourself to death trying to achieve it. A new thing is developing: our financial thinking must shift with it so that new opportunities do not leave us oblivious to their rewards. Just like the scenario with the dishwashers, we can no longer afford to remember and consider the things of old. This means reprogramming the typical Capitalism Consumer financially to win the new entrepreneurial/ social media game that is about to take over along with the economic shift. My goal is to challenge the status quo of having people under utilize their ability to manage their own finances effectively.

Every time I spend money, I want to make sure that it serves as an investment of some kind, whether it is nutrition for the body, education for the mind, clothing, transportation needs, or investment for a future standard of living.

I will admit that I am very frugal when it comes to money. Frugal is effectively defined as "economical in use or expenditure; prudently saving or sparing; not wasteful." Consumers want to tell you that being frugal is a bad thing. Don't believe the hype! Consumers only say that so that they do not have to be held accountable for what they spend. First things first: it is time to get your things in order! Every time I spend money, I want to make sure that it serves as an investment of some kind, whether it is nutrition for the body, education for the mind, clothing, transportation needs, or investment for a future standard of living. Being frugal is not the same as being cheap. I have a cousin that is cheap. Instead of buying Pepsi or Coca-Cola at the store for $1.69 for a two-liter bottle, my cousin will buy the generic brand "Kola" for $0.79. That's cheap. Frugal is getting whatever you want in a timeframe such that it does not affect your financial flow when you purchase it. If it is a major expenditure that is ultimately an investment in your needs and happiness (didn't necessarily say wants), then you plan for it, save for it, and pay for it so that when it is purchased, that is the final transaction. Remember what I said previously about credit cards. Being frugal is making sure that those "puppies" are paid off in full on or before the due date, no exceptions! There was one time that I had a Discover card with an amount due. I wrote the check for the full amount and put it in the return envelope, but somehow it ended up back in my bills folder. The next month, I received the Discover statement to find that there was a double amount due with an interest charge and late fee attached to it. That's when I discovered my inherent mistake and found the stamped envelope in the folder. I ran to the mailbox, put the bill in the mailbox, came back upstairs, and called Discover card. I told them that I received the bill and noticed that the previous month's balance payment was not recorded on the statement. They confirmed, then I told them that I put that check in the mail (which I had just done before the call). I told the lady that if they did not receive the check within the next seven days, I would send them a check for both months and cancel the check that was lost. But I needed them to credit the interest charge and the late fee to my account. After verification with her supervisor, she did just that. And that was that. No paying credit card fees- and that is non-negotiable!

This quick guide is for anyone that needs to desperately get a handle on their finances and needs a solid financial management blueprint to follow that will bring them successfully out of debt.

I am marveled at how many people I come across daily that truly lack the financial education and savvy that it takes to be successful in the investor game of Capitalism. Capitalism comes from the Latin word, 'caput,' which means to use your head. Ironically, if you don't have the financial knowledge or the means to manage your money, it is very hard to use your head to guarantee success financially. This includes being able to resolve financial conflicts between couples to preserve the family unit as well as avoiding immediate debt with the college student ambushed by credit card applications. How do you avoid these scenarios? Well, I have put together a series of course options that will give you the skills and tools to master the execution of money management and gain control of your financial future. I believe that my philosophy of money management will open the eyes of people who deeply struggle with money, whether they are living from paycheck to paycheck or are just wasting their money in all the wrong places. And I know because, at one time, I have done both.

This book is for ambitious and upcoming entrepreneurs between the ages of 18-29 who are on the fast track and need stabilization in their financial structure. This book is also for the high school student ages 15-18 that are just getting into the workforce and looking to make the most of their earnings in preparation for the college or trade transition. Finally, this book is for couples who are engaged or have been married for 7 years or less that have been having financial issues or conflicts that are stressing their marriage, whether it is paying day-to-day expenses or setting aside for their children's college education. Well, this quick guide is for anyone that needs to desperately get a handle on their finances and needs a solid financial management blueprint to follow that will bring them successfully out of debt.

There is no need to be in awe of the big money gurus like Warren Buffett, Tony Robbins, or Oprah Winfrey and what they have to say about money. Learn how to break down what they have to say and live it just like they do! I am going to help you do just that. So, let's go!

CHAPTER 1:
Do not Fall for the Money Rich Schemes and Scams

I must emphasize once again; money is very slippery. There is only one chance to hold a dollar. With that specific dollar, you can do one of two things: you can either save it and let it work for you or spend it, never to see that dollar ever again. This also includes dropping the dollar on the street, losing it altogether, spending it on some convincing get rich quick scheme, or paying for something that you don't owe. Once that dollar is gone, it is gone!

The easiness of the dollar to slip through your fingers is not solely the fault of the consumer. Businesses and their sales force are also very aware of how slippery the dollar can be and are constantly conjugating ways of getting the consumer to slip the dollar straight to them.

There is a key point to make here. The easiness of the dollar to slip through your fingers is not solely the fault of the consumer. Businesses and their sales force are also very aware of how slippery the dollar can be and are constantly conjugating ways of getting the consumer to slip the dollar straight to them. They have gotten very good at it. One method used is coming up with a quality product that they have branded so well that it becomes very difficult for the consumer to pass it up. Tumi is my brand. I love Tumi. I must confess that I have a Tumi computer bag, a Tumi 26-inch suitcase, a Tumi 22-inch suitcase, a Tumi duffle bag, a Tumi double-size suit bag, a Tumi personal accessory bag, and a Tumi golf bag! On top of that, I also have a Tumi billfold and a Tumi iPhone protector! But in my defense, I travel a lot, and the purchase of these products for me was a once-in-a-lifetime purchase. I have had my computer bag for 25 years, and I am just at the point where I must get the wheels replaced!

The brand crush is not what I am concerned about. My only advice is to make sure that your "brandaholic" purchases are not impulsive ones. The method that I am most concerned about is the disguised approaches that make great promises of doubling your income within six months, but "it takes money to make money" soon follows in the pitch. Or the disguised approach may show itself as you are in grave debt with a creditor or government agency, and if you don't pay in full within 2-12 hours, your account will be sent to legal, and the sheriff's office will be knocking on your door to arrest you for the criminal courts to prosecute you.

If you have any kind of delinquency with the IRS, they will send you a notification that will have a return receipt attached to it for you to sign stating that you received the letter and proceedings cannot start until the date you signed the receipt is verified.

This situation literally happened to me while I was in the middle of writing this chapter. It must have been a God-sent call because I have never actually had a phone call like this before. A true story/situation is given so that I can relay all the specific details to you. I had just finished eating what I would consider a perfectly cooked breakfast when I received a phone message. When I picked up my phone, the voicemail had a 202-area code attached to it. That's Washington DC. I was anticipating a call concerning my business certification, so I listened to it. It started off by saying, "This is Officer Daniel Wiseman calling you from the Legal Department of the I-R-S..."

Okay, let's stop right there. The major point here is that if you have any kind of delinquency with the IRS, they will send you a notification that will have a return receipt attached to it for you to sign stating that you received the letter and proceedings cannot start until the date you signed the receipt is verified. So, recognize the scam from the beginning. It continued by saying,

"...this is regarding a criminal lawsuit that is being filed against you. Your case reference number is CF12453, and this matter is time-sensitive, and you need to return this call. Do not disregard this message. If we don't hear from you or your attorney within the next couple of hours, then all we can do is wish you luck as the situation starts to unfold on you. Goodbye."

How did this situation fall in my lap right at this moment? The number the message told me to call back was a 314-area code. That's located in St. Louis. Since when has the IRS contacted anyone out of its St. Louis office? So, I called the number. A guy with a profound accent answered the call. He asked for my case reference number, which I gave to him. Then it was showtime. Here, in retrospect, this is how the conversation played out. First, he asked me if I would prefer to handle this matter through the court. If this was the path that I chose, then the sheriff's office would be at my house within 2 hours to arrest me, and I would be detained for 72 hours before my case would come up in court. If I wanted to handle this out of court, I would have to pay my outstanding balance of $5476. I asked where this outstanding balance came from. He told me that a letter was sent to me on 25 November 2015 and 06 February 2016, but now my case was being handed over to the criminal legal department, and my call to him was just a courtesy to handle the matter outside the court system. He then told me that if I agreed to handle this matter outside the courts, then I must stay on the phone with him until the matter was resolved. If I put him on hold, hung up the phone, or was cut off the line in any way, the matter would be closed and handed over to the courts. I had to admit that the argument given was very convincing, and it almost had me. He was very brash in his tone and extremely pushy. So, to regain my own stability, I started asking him a few questions.

First, I told him that I never received any letter from the IRS dated 25 Nov 2015 and 06 Feb 2016. Second, according to my records, the only thing that I had received from the IRS was that I got a notification that I had filed the wrong form for my LLC, which was corrected. So, what are you talking about? He said that my tax returns from 2010 thru 2015 were submitted on time but that I had several miscalculations on my forms and that the back taxes I owed amounted to $5476. I asked him if this was in penalties? He said no, this was the amount I owed from my T040 forms. T040 forms? I asked him to explain to me what a T040 form was. (Second indicator). He ignored my counter and asked me how much of the amount could I afford to pay right now? The full amount? $4000? I told him that at this point, the best I could do was $500. Then he asked me if there was a Western Union or a Walmart close to me. I said, "well, sir, before we go into that, I need to get access to these letters you told me the IRS had previously sent to me." He claimed not to have any of that information on file with him. He then started to get curt with the Walmart thing. He told me to get into my car and drive straight to Walmart. I told him that my truck was not available, and I would have to wait a few minutes before it was back. He responded that I need to take a taxi over to Walmart and wait in the parking lot for further instructions. I told him that he was crazy and way ahead of himself. First, he needed to help me get to where he was by emailing me those letters and forms that he claimed the IRS sent to me.

From my framework, I am clear of all outstanding debt owed to the IRS. Please help me understand why I owe the IRS any money whatsoever before we talk about paying at Walmart. He replied, "I didn't say anything about paying at Walmart. I said to get to Walmart as soon as possible, and I would give you further instructions." I told him, "Now you are getting ridiculous! Why else would you send me to Walmart other than to program a money order for you?" I got my tax records out. I started getting brash with him by telling him that if the amount was not a penalty, there is no way that I could possibly owe $5,476. I restated that I had never received the letters that he, for some reason, could not produce for me over email. I asked him what address the letters were sent to. He claimed that he did not have that information on file. I asked him how he could say that I received them if he didn't even have verification of the address the letters were sent to. I demanded that I needed to know the address. As he continued to resist my request, I kept quoting the amount I owed from each tax return of the years he put in question and kept making my case that there was not a possible way that I owed them anywhere near the $5476 amount he was asking for. My voice kept on an exponential crescendo until he finally gave me an address that was nowhere in the vicinity of my address with an even crazier area code. I called him on it. "You have the audacity to raise your voice at me about two IRS letters sent to me on 25 Nov 15 and 06 Feb 16, and you can't even produce the correct address these letters were sent to? Really?!" Suddenly, the phone clicked and cut off. There was no way I was going to hang up first on this conversation. The new winner has been declared!

We have all seen the schemes on the email of someone in a foreign country needing assistance to transfer an insane sum or amount that is currently being held in an offshore account, and they need your American based account to transfer the amount into offering you a cut of the money hoping that you would give them access to your account. This easy rich scheme was the first of its kind on the internet. Those emails are still floating around. But the scheme has gotten a lot better and a lot more sophisticated. Web designers have researched and found more convincing ways to convince consumers to click the button initiating the purchase. The marketers have perfected their pitch to the point that it doesn't even appear to be a pitch. Suddenly, you are in an upsell situation, ready to click that button. They prey on your financial vulnerabilities, such as questioning your financial needs in the next six months or asking what your escalating desired income is during that period. What would you like to be making per month within the next year? These types of questions serve two purposes: First, they allude to the fact that your current income amount has suddenly become insufficient. Second, greed sets in as you start to forecast your income increasing exponentially if you would just take the chance and invest with them now to secure your financial future.

My experience with one of these sophisticated schemes almost had me convinced it was the real deal even when I knew upfront that it was a scheme. It started with an arbitrary email that I received entitled, [Warren] "Buffett: BREXIT will destroy U.S. Economy-Protect Yourself." Labeled as "CNN Urgent Report: Read More," the first indicator is the statement that immediately invokes fear within the reader's psyche. By labeling it as a Warren Buffett statement, there must be truth to it, drawing the psyche in to read further. As I opened the email, the first thing that I see is what looks like a picture of Warren Buffett being interviewed by Anderson Cooper on a CNN snapshot. Of course, right below it is a big red button that says, "Read the Full Story." Curiosity kills the cat. So being intrigued, I read further. They used the interview as Buffett coming on to the show to warn the American people of the effects BREXIT is having on the economy. Then the article produced phrases such as "turmoil bad for the average American worker," "need at least $100,000 in cash in 12 months' time," and "next 3-5 years are going to be very painful." All these statements are designed to poke at the vulnerabilities of the average American middle class to alarm them that the income they make will not be enough. Finally, it talked about the four horsemen that are going to storm onto the world's economic scene where almost nothing survives. The first horsemen being "BREXIT" hurting the European economic scene. The second horsemen being "The Cash Out," making most of the world's currency become "cheap" while American money's value increases. The third horsemen being "The Collapse of U.S. Jobs" due to the undervalue of overseas currency causing U.S. companies to send their jobs overseas. The fourth horseman is the "Total Credit Destruction," with people defaulting on loans for a second go around. But the one person who has found the cure to these four horsemen is an innocent former stay-at-home mom of 2 kids who needs to make enough money to put food on the table.

I called myself being responsible checking out my "Budgeting in THREE Dimensions" spreadsheet.

Although these items brought up for discussion may be legitimate concerns as it could lead to something worse than the recession of 2008, the solution to all of your worries was the click that took you to a site where "regular people were becoming millionaires in a matter of months." If only the readers were to take advantage, they could get far more than they need to survive the coming global chaos. Now I am extremely vulnerable to this oncoming crisis that I know good and well that I am not prepared for (need at least $100,000 in cash in 12 months' time). What else can I do but click the button? Plus, there is a rush because space is limited, and they can only accept a few more applicants. The offer expires the following day of the article. So, I clicked. I filled out my information and clicked the button that gave them permission to check for availability. Of course, it comes back and lets me know that there are only 12 slots left in my zip code region. Then comes the "oh by the way..." You must "pay in" in order to "get in." Only $97! (was $199) And by the way, the 12 slots have gone down to only 3 slots left. No time left to ponder over the issue. Must decide NOW!!

Wow! I can feel the vulnerabilities ganging up on me internally. There is not much time! Need to move on this. I called myself being responsible and checking out my "Budget-Cubed" spreadsheet" (remember this phrase, we will get to it) to see where that $97 could come from as this now seems to be categorized under an emergency for funding. Postpone my plane ticket purchase, cut back on my grocery bill for the month, tell my daughter that we will have to wait on that new phone I promised her- crazy moves at the last minute to make this opportunity happen. Besides, it promises to make my return on investment within six months at the most. So once again, I click the button, this time with my credit card information preceding the click.

Congratulations! I am officially in the club and have access to all the website information available to new members. I scan the information over and start reading how I am going to suddenly make that $100,000 over the next 12 months to overcome the travesty soon to hit the financial markets. As I am reviewing the information and watching the videos, I receive an email instructing me to call an 866 number for the program. So, I called and got their customer service. The representative gave me the typical congratulation speech for taking this major step in becoming a member of the program. His assignment was to put me in touch with a specialist who was going to guide me through the rest of the program. If I could stand by for 30 minutes, the specialist would contact me. Sure, I have gotten this far. I can certainly wait another 30 minutes. I hung up and continued watching the videos online. Almost to the exact second before 30 minutes, the specialist calls from Utah. Congratulations once again for becoming a "doer" as opposed to just being a "talker." I have entered the arena of direct marketing (not sure if I really knew that prior to this moment). He asked if I could dedicate 10 hours per week to the effort; if I was open-minded to be able to follow the guidance of the experts on staff, and of course, money! However, the talk of the money went from making whatever amount I desired per month to the strategy of using my credit card money to get started and paying it back, never having to touch my own money. Could I be a decision-maker on this? My response to him was that I could give him a yes or no answer once I see what the program is and determine if it is truly for me. He didn't like that response. He told me that if he would have to recommend me to the "director," and he would need a yes or no answer as soon as the conversation was finished. We went back and forth on this issue for a little bit. Finally, I told him that if all my questions were answered during the conversation, then I would be willing to give him a yes or no answer by the end. That was my ticket of recommendation by the specialist to the director. The specialist asked if I could be available in the next hour and fifteen minutes to speak to the director. This takes my waiting over two hours to get into this program. Sure, why not. So once again, I waited.

At exactly one hour and fifteen minutes, I get a call from the director out of Seattle. As soon as we start, he tells me that he received high recommendations on my behalf from each of the previous correspondents that I spoke with. Then came how much you would like to make within the next six months. So, I told him how much would be enough. The next question was how much I would be willing to invest in order to make it happen. What do you mean by that? Well, if I was willing to invest $15-20K, I would get access to all of the tools they provide to work aggressively to achieve my goal; $10-15K would provide a moderate path to obtaining my goals; and $6-10K would be a conservative approach to making the six-month goal. For $6000, I would have access to the software, the relationships with potential customers, and the search engine optimization (SEO) that they would provide for me to get my website and products out to the customer base. On top, he was going to send me a contract warranty of service, which guaranteed that if I did my part, their system would not fail. But I had to pay $6000 right there.

Now let's pull back for a second. This all started with an article about the collapse of the U.S. Economy to where unemployment would grow to 50%. Next, I was paying $97 to be a part of the solution apparently endorsed by Warren Buffett, but first, I had to add an additional investment using my credit cards as the initial down payment. Oh, by the way, that amount would be $20,000, but for you, you can start with just $6,000. Wow. Okay. I didn't get to check my "Budget-Cubed" spreadsheet this time. My vulnerability is at an all-time high. Just do it. So, I gave the director my credit card information for a one-time payment of $6000. He congratulates me for taking this gigantic step and promises that I would be their testimonial once I reached my six-month goal. Now I just needed to wait another 15 minutes to speak with my specialist to make sure that we were all on the same page.

Emotional vulnerability, particularly when it comes to financial opportunities, is a very delicate moment, and a lot of companies are looking to prey on these very vulnerabilities when you least expect it.

My emotions were all over the place. First, all the videos that I had reviewed before talking to the director were suddenly nullified by him as being a junk website for members who were trying to do this on their own. But since I had paid the $6000, I would have access to their exclusive information and experts to help me perform my tasks. The only problem was I still didn't have a clear view of what I really was signing up to do. But I had enrolled, so to speak. 15 minutes later, the specialist called me and told me that he had just sent me an email with a link for payment. Hmm, didn't the director just take my payment information? Oh, the link is for me to send my purchase request to the credit card company on their behalf.

What he didn't realize is that I had put a block on my credit card to keep significant purchases from going through. He insisted that he would call the credit card company on a three-way conference call to straighten out the whole thing. I wasn't happy about it at all. Not only did he call the number, but once customer service came on the line, he spoke over me to declare who he was and that I was his client trying to complete the transaction. The bully posture was in full effect. The credit card company turned us over to the fraud and abuse department. He once again orchestrated the call on his behalf. But the department would not let him stay on the line due to my sensitive information. He had to hang up, and I called the credit card back. When I spoke to the representative, she informed me that prior to our call, they had already tried to submit a charge for $3000 on two separate occasions, that their company was registered as an international company, and that they had no official U.S. address associated with their merchant service. Clearly, they were a high-risk entity as far as my charge investment was concerned. I called the representative back and told him that due to the recent events, I was going to withdraw my application to work on their behalf. He made every maneuver he could to keep me on the line, including making another call with the director. "This will be a once-in-a-lifetime opportunity." Now I was just getting mad. "I will pass on this once-in-a-lifetime opportunity."

The key to successful money management is consistency, discipline, time, and motivation.

The key point I would like to make here is that it should have been crystal clear that this development was a scam. Emotional vulnerability, particularly when it comes to financial opportunities, is a very delicate moment, and a lot of companies are looking to prey on these very vulnerabilities when you least expect it. When it started, all I was doing was reading a controversial article; the next thing I know, I was paying a program entrance fee and facing an upsell almost immediately. Awareness is critical to avoiding falling victim to such an incident.

One of the key aspects of money management is to understand that accumulating wealth has nothing to do with how much you make in a week's or a month's period. The key to successful money management is consistency, discipline, time, and motivation. Understanding this fact keeps you from becoming a possible victim of the "six-month change' to your financial life and situation. This is not to negate that you can change your whole financial situation in six months. However, you will be in control of the decision of how your initial investments need to be distributed as opposed to someone else doing it for you.

CHAPTER 2:
Become A Financial Steward

Declaration: *Today is the Day that I take control of my financial responsibility and destiny as God would have me to do!*

I believe that God's primary purpose and wish for all of us is to be prosperous and of a giving spirit to others sharing his glory to all who we interact with on a day-to-day basis. It was not his purpose for us to experience any kind of poverty or poor conditions. It says it clear in III John 3:2-4:

Beloved, I pray that you may prosper in all things and be in health, just as your soul prospers. For I rejoiced greatly when brethren came and testified of the truth that is in you, just as you walk in the truth. I have no greater joy than to hear that my children walk in truth.

If it wasn't God's intent for us to experience poverty, to have versus to have not, to walk in truth instead of chaos and confusion, then why is it that only 1 out of 850 people become financially independent and successful in their own right? Why have the other 849 people faltered away from having financial empowerment and dwell within struggle from living day to day?

It is a known fact that our tendencies to shop and spend money impulsively are directly correlated to emotional responses, particularly to depression, anxiety, frustration, and sadness.

KRS-One spoke eloquently in one of his famous songs in the 1990s, where he mentions, "Visualize wealth and put yourself in the picture." This is a very important emphasis as it speaks to the fact that wealth must be created in the mind before it can come into fruition and especially if you plan to sustain wealth. Wealth is not just in the form of money. As a matter of fact, a lot of money is not needed to create wealth. We only need time, discipline, focus, and motivation to create it. Unfortunately, the majority of the 849 people are easily distracted from wealth creation. Society loves to distract the consumer and markets above and beyond to get those 849 people distracted and spending. To spend in this manner is to start our wealth creation from scratch. If I get my paycheck at the end of the week on a Friday and I go and spend all but the rent money over the weekend on the club scene, shopping malls, dining out, etc., I have just started my wealth creation all over again. In addition, it cannot start until the next paycheck arrives. Our insecurities often perpetuate a tendency to sabotage our wealth creation. It is a known fact that our tendencies to shop and spend money impulsively are directly correlated to emotional responses, particularly to depression, anxiety, frustration, and sadness. Thus, if I buy something, it will help my mood. Ironically, once the mood finally changes, we realize that the very thing that we bought to help our mood no longer has any use to us and becomes a coffee table paperweight, and wealth creation is put on hold.

You can have anything you want, but you cannot have everything you want.

If wealth creation is to become, we must gain control of our impulsive spending habits. My motto in my house is that you can have anything you want, but you cannot have everything. Anything you want must be planned for. If you see it and you want it, refrain from purchasing it instantaneously. Come home, review the budget, and see what can be shuffled around so that the next day, you can go back to purchase it. However, that means something else on the budget must wait. You can't do both. This is where the discipline and focus have their impact. Sometimes, the thing that you want must wait until the next month when you can put it into the budget accordingly. Otherwise, it is guaranteed that your wealth creation will be compromised.

All the long-term planning in the world will not be worth two cents if we don't save and invest. That will turn 'you can have anything' to 'you have absolutely nothing!'

The other thing that compromises our path to wealth creation is the myth that we can have it all. This has the capability to increase our desires but is detrimental to our pocketbook. Some people even feel that they are entitled to have it all. The reality is that the laws of supply and demand will not allow us to have it all, no matter how hard we work. So, long-term planning is vital if we are to become a financial steward. Wealth creation in making a comfortable retirement may mean that we have to forego getting the luxury car and stick with a small pickup truck. Wealth creation by investing in our startup business may mean foregoing a wardrobe full of high-end clothing and suits. Wealth creation in saving to make sure that our kids get into a top private school ultimately receiving a quality college education may mean that we must forego buying the big house with two acres. My oldest daughter's yearly tuition at one of the top schools in the country went from $57,000 per year her freshman year to a mere $65,000 per year her senior year. The inflation of college tuition and fees has increased by 1,375% since the year 1978. But it is worth the investment for our children. My point here is that there is no one good or bad choice. Whatever choice we decide to pursue, impulsive spending damages our opportunity to achieve it. The reality is many people talk about it but never actually become serious savers. They squander their money and time because they never learn to gain discipline and focus on reducing the profligate spending that takes place. All the long-term planning in the world is not worth two cents if we don't save and invest. That will turn 'you can have anything' to 'you have absolutely nothing!'

Wealth creation comes in two forms: financial wealth and spiritual wealth. The two forms are interdependent of each other. Most people only want to focus on financial wealth in order to live the life that is worth living. Well, there are several people that are doing just that; they are filthy rich yet are not wealthy and still very unhappy. Why is that? Because they have neglected the aspects of spiritual wealth, they are not able to find fulfillment within their life. So, both are necessary. I refer to the combination of the two as Self Wealth. God wants us to be engulfed in Self Wealth in every possible way: Physically, mentally, spiritually, socially, which translates into health, love, peace of mind, and yes, material possessions. Matthew 6:33 states:

"But seek first the kingdom of God and His righteousness, and all these things shall be added to you."

Our goal should be to become stewards of financial and spiritual wealth. As our awareness of financial wealth integrates with spiritual wealth, a loop of free flow starts to create an investment of ourselves and our finances that glorifies God. People will start to see God through us, our time, our sacrifices, and our giving. If we neglect either component, our self-wealth goes bankrupt.

The neglect of budgeting our money over the course of time is directly correlated, in my opinion, with gambling.

Luke 16:10-11 says, He who is faithful in what is least is faithful also in much; and he who is unjust in what is least is unjust also in much. Therefore, if you have not been faithful in the unrighteous mammon, who will commit to your trust the true riches.

God's trust of true riches comes when we can demonstrate faithfully that we are responsible stewards and that he can trust us with a little so he can trust us with a lot. So being appreciative when God gives us a little and becoming a steward with that little ultimately leads to being appreciative when God gives us a lot and becoming a steward with a lot. That is the growth of Self Wealth and being trustworthy of not blowing the lot impulsively.

Speaking of impulsive, another menace to becoming a financial steward is the emotion of gambling. Yes, this includes the compulsion of going to Las Vegas for the chance at instant financial gratification. But the form of gambling that I am primarily focusing on is the lack of budgeting in households. Money is very slippery. The neglect of budgeting our money over the course of time is directly correlated, in my opinion, with gambling. Without budgeting, we are basically taking a 1 in 1,000,000 shot that our money will work for us and make us successful. If we get to the end of the month or the end of a pay period and can't account for half of the income we made and where it was spent, we are gambling for tough times financially in the long term. Having a budgeting process is critical to becoming a financial steward. Even so, most people who do put forth the effort to execute some form of a budget process do not necessarily have an effective one. My purpose is to demonstrate a highly effective budget process that will not only help see where our money is being spent but also highlight areas where we can afford to reduce our spending to convert that money into investment opportunities. It also helps reduce the amount of bad debt that we may have accumulated over time and strategize ways to become debt-free. Budgeting is the process of converting our financial status from poverty to prosperity. Once budgeting becomes a discipline, investing becomes the tool to bring prosperity into our reality. Creating and managing our portfolio enables us to achieve wealth. Once we achieve wealth, estate and tax planning allow us to keep our wealth, and insurance keeps us from losing our wealth. The objective here is to learn the skills and tools of investing effectively and then sharing these investment principles with someone else so that they can transform their habits as consumers over to that of investors.

Budgeting is the process of converting our financial status from poverty to prosperity. Once budgeting becomes a discipline, investing becomes the tool to bring prosperity into our reality.

In order to become a true financial steward, we must be convinced that God has a purpose for our lives and will work to guide us through it. It is my opinion that nothing happens by chance. Everything that happens is a lesson to prepare us for a specific purpose in the future. That purpose will have an impact on someone else in the future. That is why patience and persistence are so important to becoming a financial steward. No matter what circumstances take place in life, the focus has to stay the same. Perseverance as a financial steward is dependent on it.

"Words that you speak, manifest into your future, then they become!"

One of the biggest obstacles that we must overcome is becoming aware of all the statements that have been made since childhood about money. The statements that we heard when we were young have an effect on our financial life. Words that you speak, or you allow to be spoken to you manifest into your future, then they become. Sayings such as "Money is the root of all evil," or "Money doesn't matter," or "You shouldn't focus on money" bring on negative connotations that will incrementally grow to become a part of our reality. People that constantly repeat these types of phrases start to wonder why when the time comes that they need money, they can never find it as it seems to run away from them. Sayings such as "Well, I'm broke anyway, so I might as well spend the little bit that I have" or "You only live once..." become justifications or rationale for letting go and ruthlessly spending everything they have. Let's face it, for most of us, going on a shopping spree with 'irrational exuberance' is a lot of fun. But reckless spending is the enemy of becoming a financial steward. Do not believe the hype of those money clichés. Money may not be considered everything, but I will guarantee that its importance is right up there with water and, ultimately, oxygen. We have to drink it and breathe it, or life will quickly be cut short. Health problems can have a routine cure if money is available. If money is not there, a routine health problem can accumulate on itself and suddenly become life-threatening. So, it is important to take a holistic approach to establishing and maintaining our financial health and to keeping it strong no matter how awry the economy may be. I believe that using declarations and reciting them out loud helps tremendously in disassociating from negative saying, and they allow us to realign with positive sayings that are more fitting for us in commencing our financial journey.

Reckless spending is the enemy of becoming a financial steward.

Just in case you are not sure what would serve as a fitting declaration for your current situation, I would like to quickly review some key points that come from T. Harv Eker's book, Secrets of the Millionaire Mind: Mastering the Inner Game of Wealth. Eker digs down into the mental state differentials between people who dwell in prosperity and people who flock towards poverty. There are five major points that I would like to reiterate here. As we go through these, we will be able to formulate the types of declarations to recite that will ultimately turn your financial state around.

Rich people always say, "I create my life." Poor people always say, "Life happens to me." (Eker, SECRETS, pp. 54)

In the beginning, God created the heavens and the earth. When God created Man, He created man in His own image. That means we have the capacity and the power to create. God has granted us this journey call life and has given us the brush to paint it. We can create what life is supposed to be with the resources that the universe has provided for us. Unfortunately, there are a lot of people who prefer (whether consciously or subconsciously) to complain, blame, or justify why life has happened to them, looking for sympathy in the process. In the meantime, they allow other people to dictate their lives for them.

Declaration: "I will not blame, complain, or justify my situation!"

1) Rich people are committed to being rich. Poor people want to be rich. (Eker, SECRETS, pp. 65)

It is so easy to sit back and say, "If only I had a million dollars, I would..." I can guarantee that there is not one person on this planet that doesn't want to have money. The difference is that most people only will sit back and talk about it while continuing to impulsively spend the little bit of money they have. Want by itself will not suffice to get you to the wealthy category. There is a commitment that must be sustained in a disciplined fashion if you ever want to obtain that status.

Declaration: I will sacrifice impulsive short-term desires for long-term financial gain!

2) Rich people act in spite of fear. Poor people let fear stop them. (Eker, SECRETS, pp. 166)

Success can be a scary thing! Success is a prerequisite for a life-changing situation. Do you really want your life to change from what you are familiar with? Fear is one of the strongest human emotions and has the capability to stop you in your tracks. If you allow fear to stop you from creating your life, your failures turn into "quits" instead of "wrong outcomes." If it becomes a "quit," there is no further pursuit. If it becomes a "wrong outcome," it becomes necessary to move forward to find the "right outcome."

Declaration: I will always act in spite of fear and fail my way to success!

3) Rich people focus on opportunities. Poor people focus on obstacles. (Eker, SECRETS, pp. 78)

When I speak of opportunities vs. obstacles, I immediately think about the predicament of Mary Magdalene in Mark 16:1-4:

Now when the Sabbath was past, Mary Magdalene, Mary the mother of James, and Salome bought spices, that they might come and anoint Him. 2 Very early in the morning, on the first day of the week, they came to the tomb when the sun had risen. 3 And they said among themselves, "Who will roll away the stone from the door of the tomb for us?" 4 But when they looked up, they saw that the stone had been rolled away—for it was very large.

The opportunity here was for the three ladies to go to the tomb and anoint the body of Jesus Christ, who had been crucified. The obstacle was the large stone in front of the tomb. What if Mary Magdalene, Mary, and Salome, having to carry the hundred pounds of spices all the way to the gravesite, had focused on the stone, determined that they couldn't move it, and decided to stay at home instead of carrying all of those spices just to the turnaround? If they had focused on that obstacle, they would have never received the blessing at the tomb and the opportunity to be the first witnesses of the resurrection.

Declaration: I will present myself every day to receive the opportunities that life has chosen to give to me in spite of the obstacles!

4) Rich people constantly learn and grow. Poor people think they already know. (Eker, SECRETS, pp. 179)

Life is a continuous journey of learning, and new experiences are encountered every day. No matter how long we may have played a game or worked a job, something new will always happen that we have never experienced before. We should make it an objective to constantly learn and better ourselves along the way. The only thing that can stop us from learning and growing is when we put our foot down and say, "I already know that." That expression is nothing more than a defensive mechanism that attempts to give the illusion that we have more knowledge than everyone else. The only problem is that no one else is affected by that posture. Even if we already know, we should always be open to better or more efficient ways of doing the same thing. I often hear the term being "coachable." Everyone needs to have a coach along the lines of where we need to learn and grow.

Declaration: I will always remain coachable so that I can constantly learn and grow!

Chapter 3:

Give!

I was attending a Sunday school class on a crisp fall morning, and the instructor made a profound statement that resonated with me so much that I realized that this book would not be complete unless I expounded on it in full detail; thus, this chapter was born. The instructor said that the sign of a true man is one that dwells within delayed gratification. He makes sure that the needs of his family and other people that are dependents within his circle are taken care of before he takes care of his own personal vendettas. I found this to be so true. When my daughters were young, I was constantly shuffling around resources for my family that were originally supposed to be for me. Money at the beginning of the month for my pleasure trip became something they needed as the month progressed. I made a habit of waiting to cash in any budget items that were for me until the end of the month. Most of the time that would result in having to wait until the next month to make my pleasure purchase. But that was okay as I knew that I was diligent in providing for my family.

The sign of a true man is one that dwells within delayed gratification.

The instructor gave us an example of an experience he had witnessed that was contrary to the matter. I really appreciated it when he would give life examples he had experienced in the class. He came from a totally different background and experience than me. He used to be a pastor of a small country church in Tennessee, and they had a program where they would conduct outreach into the community to help and give to those in need. One Thanksgiving week, they had prepared several bags of groceries to give out to families so that they could have a full Thanksgiving meal. Each bag had everything that a family would need to cook the whole meal, from the turkey to the spices for seasoning. He recalled going to this one house in a trailer park that pretty much resembled an outhouse in a middle of an unkempt field. They walked up to the house, and there was a man with his wife and three kids living in a place that he considered unfit for human occupancy. The man invited him to enter the compound, and he noticed that the kids were running around outside and through the house wearing only diapers and dirty clothes. Their ages appeared to be 5, 3, and 14 months old. He felt embarrassed as he asked the man where he would like for them to put the turkey and the supporting ingredients for the Thanksgiving dinner. The man, who sat back down on his couch in front of his 52" television screen, nonchalantly told him to put the turkey in the refrigerator. Now my instructor noticed that the man had several elaborate tattoos on his arm, his carton of cigarettes next to the couch with an ashtray loaded with cigarette butts as if he was a chain smoker, and a six-pack of beer next to the cigarettes. As he opened the refrigerator to put the turkey in, he noticed that the only thing that was in the refrigerator was another six-pack of beer and a half-full container of mashed potatoes from Kentucky Fried Chicken. There was no food, milk, or Kool-Aid in the refrigerator that would support the basic needs of his family. Now, I have never gone to a tattoo parlor before, but from what I understand, an elaborate tattoo like the one he had cost a pretty penny. Plus, the cost of cigarettes and beer, let alone the 52" LCD screen and the huge dish that sat outside of the house, is substantial enough to raise major concern as to why he purchased those things, but his family did not have any clothes given that it was quite cold on that day in November. Where is the food for his family? Why is he satisfied to keep his family in that house? One thing that is vital in becoming a financial steward is to get our financial priorities in order. This man is a prime example of what not to do.

Our willingness to give in the service of others completes the cycle of wealth.

The lesson from this story is we need to have a giving spirit. Our ability to effectively manage our financials directly correlate to becoming wealthy economically, but more so spiritually. Our willingness to give in the service of others completes the cycle of wealth. But giving is more than just money; it is giving of

ourselves, our gifts, and our time to help others in need. If we allow our spirits to enter this realm, it helps us find our purpose in life and how our gifts are to be of benefit for the whole world for God's glory. Once we find this purpose, the resources that we need to execute our purpose becomes endless. But it all starts with giving. Luke 6:38 states,
"Give, and it will be given to you: good measure, pressed down, shaken together, and running over will be put into your bosom. For with the same measure that you use, it will be measured back to you."

There have been numerous inquiries over the difference between rich and wealthy. I have heard various answers to this inquiry that may or may not represent itself in the physical realm being that rich is having a lot of money while still working versus wealthy is having a lot of money to the point of never having to work again. Okay, if you say so, but after a lot of deep thought and struggle going through the course of the 2016 presidential election, I came to realize the true answer to this question. What is the difference between being rich and being wealthy? If you don't get anything else out of this quick guide, be sure to grab this: Being RICH is having a lot of money without a purpose in life other than one that is self-fulfilling. However, being WEALTHY is having a lot of money with a mindset of giving and the purpose of giving to help others in such a way that your gifts are aligned, giving God the glory! The purpose of this quick guide is to gift to you the skills and tools that you will need to transform your mindset to that of a wealthy place to embalm yourself within God's swirly, spiritual movement.

Being RICH is having a lot of money with no purpose in life other than those that are self-fulfilling. However, being WEALTHY is having a lot of money with a mindset of giving and the purpose of giving to help others in the special way your gifts are aligned that will ultimately give God glory!

Let me sum it up in two paragraphs. Because the rich have no purpose other than self-fulfilling ones, they, being the narcissistic people that they are, will align themselves in positions of power so that they can give the illusion of ruling over people in poverty so that it is all about them. Why people in poverty? People in poverty are ignorant to the fact that they have power; they believe the only way to have power is to have money. They do not know that there is a difference. They end up submitting to people who have money as if they are in awe of them and fall into their trap accordingly. Unfortunately, they later realize that the rich they are submitting to do not have their interest at heart because they are solely in self-fulfilling mode. Therefore, the people in poverty only see more poverty. Their lives are in disarray and out of order. They have no knowledge of money and how money works. Impoverished people often fail to realize the little pocket change they do have can be transformed into wealth if they were to align themselves in God's will accordingly. It's like going to a self-serving car wash, and the meter takes your money, but the car wash doesn't turn on the water and soap for you to wash your car. If you are spiritually "out of order," it is impossible for you to be invested in. Decide today not to be in poverty!

How does that differ from the motive of the WEALTHY? The wealthy also tends to have a lot of money. Only with them, it is not about the money. It is about the people that they can help with the riches that they have afforded. For this example, I must mention Bill Gates. According to Forbes for the year 2016, he was ranked #1 on the World's Top 10 billionaires with a net worth of $75 billion. I had the opportunity to hear the current president of the Bill Gates Foundation speak at an Economic Development Corporation breakfast in San Diego. He said that the Bill Gates Foundation looks for someone or something to invest in that doesn't make money on their behalf but makes a tremendous "impact" on people that need it. The keyword is "impact," such that they are not looking to invest in something that will treat HIV and AIDS but will "cure" it. If it doesn't fit that description, they will wait until a need comes along that does. Why is this important? Bill Gates is wealthy because he gives to help others in need, and ultimately, the gifts come right back to him such that he doesn't have to work for it anymore. What does Luke 6:38 say on the previous page? Bill Gates is the example that fits wealthy. I will let you decide who is the example that fits being rich.

God is a spirit. A spirit is constantly in movement. Its movement is of a spinning nature which resembles a circular flow. God, being the creator, has passed his spinning nature onto us. Our physical nature is of a spinning nature. For instance, our hair has spinning characteristics. Kinky hair curves as it grows out to where if you were to pull it out, it would curl into a little ball as you hold it in your hand. Even if you have straight hair, your hairline demonstrates either a clockwise or counterclockwise flow to it. As we open our hands, it opens into a golden spiral from the pinky to the thumb. Yet, our spirit is a spinning force. That is why it's hard to remain stagnant or stationary when it comes to our spiritual growth. Giving helps to maintain momentum in God's spiritual flow. God finds favor in your giving and creates ways to send you gifts in overflow as a result of your giving. However, if you are giving and helping others stop flowing, that cuts off the wormhole that brings blessings to you. I can attest to both scenarios.

If we allow God's light to shine through us on any given day, someone who encounters our space will receive a blessing from us.

There was a time that I hosted a Pampered Chef party for the fellas. I noticed that a lot of single men had refrigerators that only hosted containers that had restaurant logos on them. Usually, that means that person is not eating a well-balanced diet, especially when all you see is a Wendy's soda cup or a Kentucky Fried Chicken big box. My goal was to demonstrate how simple it was to cook a very basic but nutritional meal using basic pots and stones from Pampered Chef. The party was well attended by members of my church and a few friends from work and the neighborhood. We baked a chicken in a roasting stone using onions and celery. We also made a simple vegetable omelet using slow cook and a frying pan. At the end of the show, only one of the guys bought a set of steak knives. This threw off the lady that was hosting the Pampered Chef for me as she couldn't believe that only one person bought something right after the show. I made a note to her that this was an all men's showing, which is quite different from when women attend. I told her not to worry. The reason was men take the time to go home, review the information they received and the value it has in changing their lives for the better. This often happens with the women in their lives. Once they determine how to best implement that value, they will respond accordingly. Sure enough, one week later, we received a ton of orders, and the Pampered Chef representative informed me that our show was one of the highest-grossing events she had ever hosted. That meant a lot of cooking accessories for me.

It felt good giving my cooking advice to people who were limping along on Pizza Hut boxes and Taco Bell wrappers.

God created us in Our own image. To me, that means that our pure presence can be a blessing in helping others. If we allow God's light to shine through us on any given day, someone who encounters our space will receive a blessing from us. Our desire to submit and give to this cause is a guarantee that God's favor will find us on a pass-through in the future. God wants us to posture on this wave of submitting and giving in all aspects of our lives. We should be willing to submit and give to our authorities at work. We should be willing to submit and give to our subordinates as well. We should be willing to submit and give to our families with "storge" love. We should be willing to submit and give to God as the creator of us. Finally, we should be willing to submit and give to our spouses or significant others in our marital and romantic relationships.

Ephesians 5:22-28 talks about the essence of husbands loving your wives and wives submitting to your husbands.

22 Wives submit to your own husbands, as to the
Lord. 23 For the husband is head of the wife, as also
Christ is head of the church; and He is the Savior of
the body. 24 Therefore, just as the church is subject to
Christ, so let the wives be to their own husbands in
everything.
25 Husbands, love your wives, just as Christ also loved
the church and gave Himself for her, 26 that He might
sanctify and cleanse her with the washing of water by

the word, 27(that He might present her to Himself a glorious church, not having spot or wrinkle or any such thing, but that she should be holy and without blemish. 28 So husbands ought to love their own wives as their own bodies; he who loves his wife loves himself.

My question is, "why doesn't it say the reverse: Wives love your husbands and husbands submit to your wives?" My response is not what you may think. I believe that the reason Ephesians states it the way that it does is because it serves as a commandment of what we are most likely not to uphold. By that I mean that it is more of a natural state for men to submit to their wives than it is to love them. Loving for men must be purposeful and deliberate, just like Christ was purposeful and deliberate in loving the church. However, men submit to their wives and their families all the time. Earlier, we referred to a true man as dwelling in delayed gratification. The same goes for the man who accompanies his wife shopping when he would much prefer staying home to watch the ball game. On the other hand, it is a natural and nurturing thing for women to love. However, when you bring up submitting, women want to stay away from the conversation about being submissive at all costs. Submitting for women must be purposeful and deliberate. But I will say that nowhere does it say that women need to submit to foolishness. So, as women posture in their decision to submit, men must posture in their decision to love. If God placed man as the head of the household in this capacity and woman is the helpmate, that means the woman is accountable, but the man is responsible. For a relationship to function and grow as God intended, both members must be able to both love and submit to one another, which is a token of giving to each other.

Giving is good for the heart, mind, and soul. But, the divine law is that in order for someone to give, there has to be someone to receive. So, in addition to the need for us to be great givers, we also have to learn how to be great receivers. The art of giving and receiving flows in God's process to where our giving and receiving contributes to something much bigger than we are. Our gifts become blessings to others when we fully engage ourselves in giving. Many people love to give of themselves, but they are very poor receivers. When offered gifts that were unexpected, you often hear them expressing, "Oh, I can't accept this. It's too expensive." They will also reject gifts being given to them because they feel that somehow it demotes them in class status if they accept the gifts. But it is a blessing to be in a position to give to someone. So how can you possibly deny others the opportunity to give to you? Be a cheerful giver, but in equivalence, be a cheerful receiver. Let God use you to be a blessing to someone else. If you allow God to give a blessing through you, God will find a way to get a blessing to you.

Chapter 4:

Budget! Budget! Budget! (Budgeting in THREE Dimensions)

This is the portion where we really define how to be effective with our money management to accomplish our financial goals. Can we make our money work for us no matter how little or how much money we have? Are we capable of creating new financial opportunities by changing our mindset and treating our money differently? The answer is yes. Our journey is to pinpoint how to develop a money portfolio that is based on your financial goals, your age, and your level of risk tolerance. In order to do that, we first must understand the seven methodical steps to create wealth:

<u>The Seven Methodical Steps to Creating Capital for Investment</u>
(Robbins, MONEY, pp. 249-368)

1) Increase Your Income and Allocate Assets
2) Reduce Your Expenses and Invest the Difference
3) Reduce Your Taxes & Fees and Invest the Difference
4) Save More and Invest the Difference
5) Earn More and Invest the Difference

6) Get Better Returns thru Diversified Portfolios
7) Don't Lose Money

First, I will point out that four of the seven outlooks contain the phrase, "Invest the Difference."
This phrase implies we must find disciplined ways to extract money from the amount we already have to invest in order to increase our financial portfolio.
This will require thinking about our money differently.
This will require changing how we spend our money, and the emotional grip spending money has on our everyday lives. Are you up for the challenge?

My budgeting philosophy is built on the premise that the budget process comes in three phases: Projected Budget, Actual Budget, and Summary Budget. In other words, "Budgeting in THREE Dimensions!"

Are you serious about accomplishing this drastic change in lifestyle? Are you serious about sacrificing in the short term to have abundance in the long term? If so, this will require incorporating the principles of the seven methodical outlooks listed above.

1) Increase Your Income and Allocate Assets- Clearly, the best way to find money is to increase your income. What does allocate assets mean to you? When most people finally get a raise, the first thing they do is find a new way to spend it. It is almost like they didn't get a raise at all. My philosophy is

to allocate your raises before you receive them. Your current lifestyle does not have to change immediately after you receive a raise. In some cases, it is best to allocate all the raise to increasing your investments. However, you must be the best judge in determining how your assets need to be allocated. And your mindset will determine what you do with it. Save it, invest it or spend it.

2) Reduce Your Expenses and Invest the Difference- There are two ways to generate and/or free up capital. Either we can increase our income as mentioned in the first outlook, or we can reduce expenses to free up capital. That means finding a way to lower our bills by reducing your gas & electric bills, find ways to reduce household costs or decrease transportation and insurance costs.
If we are successful in decreasing any of these expenses, we can turn them into investment capital.

3) Reduce Your Taxes & Fees and Invest the Difference- Taxes on average can account for 33% of our income. By paying attention to the tax laws and implementing tax strategies to ensure that we legally reduce our tax rates with tax deductions, bringing that 33% down

to 15% surely frees up income that can be invested.

4) Save More and Invest the Difference- If we resist the temptation of spending more, that translates into saving more. Conscious spending helps to facilitate saving. This is the most accessible way to create investment capital.

5) Earn More and Invest the Difference- This outlook is very similar to the first one. By creating multiple streams of income outside of just your primary job helps you earn more using your gifts and talents to help others will bring investment capital.

6) Get Better Returns thru Diversified Portfolios- This is where learning how to manage our money and diversifying our investment portfolio pays off. If we create an investing model that will allow us to profit no matter what season the economy is in, the returns made will help us accomplish our financial goals.

7) Don't Lose Money! - Words of the wise coming from Warren Buffet. What does that exactly mean? If we are not managing our bills such that we are constantly paying finance charges and/or late fees, we are

losing money. If we find ourselves going out and impulsively spending for emotional needs instead of buying essential needs, we are losing money. If we look at every expenditure made during the month, we should ask ourselves, "Is this expenditure a true investment in something meaningful?" If not, then we are losing money. If we are careless about traffic laws and constantly receiving traffic parking tickets or speeding tickets, we are losing money. Don't lose money!

How do we keep from losing money? How do we find excess capital to invest when money is so tight? My answer is Budget, Budget, Budget, better known as Budget^3 (Budgeting in THREE Dimensions)! Budgeting is the tool that we use to incorporate the seven methodical outlooks. Budgeting is the means where we can gain control of our finances without having control! So how is it that having a simple budget can change your whole financial outlook, but so many people fail to budget successfully? How is it that so many people have financial conflicts because they cannot agree on a budget to move forward with? Well, this chapter will define the solution for you.

The primary reason most people fail at budgeting is that they attempt to budget at the beginning of the period that they are budgeting for all in one step. This never works because once the period starts, it is inevitable that an emergency, some unexpected expense, or a shortage of income occurs, which will throw the budgeting process completely out of sync. People then get frustrated and give up, which is the worst thing to do. My budgeting philosophy is built on the premise that the budget process comes in three phases: Projected Budget, Actual Budget, and Summary Budget. In other words, Budgeting in THREE Dimensions! (See Chart #1)

Chart #1: Budgeting in THREE Dimensions Worksheet

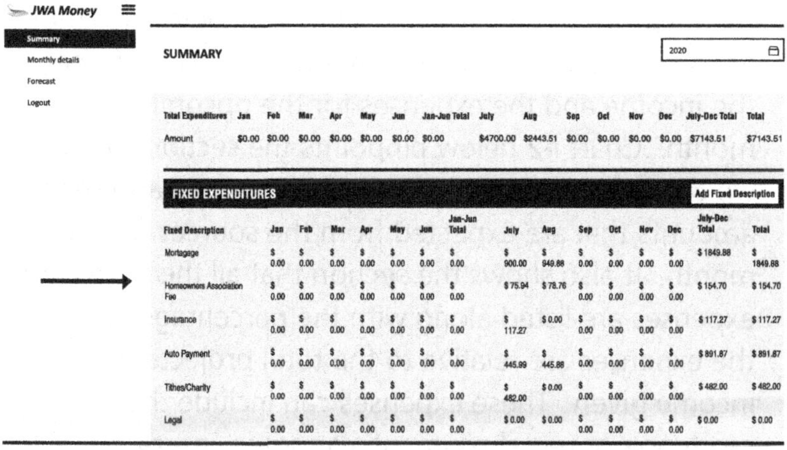
JWA Money

Summary
Monthly details
Forecast
Logout

SUMMARY

2020

Total Expenditures	Jan	Feb	Mar	Apr	May	Jun	Jan-Jun Total	July	Aug	Sep	Oct	Nov	Dec	July-Dec Total	Total
Amount	$0.00	$0.00	$0.00	$0.00	$0.00	$0.00	$0.00	$4700.00	$2443.51	$0.00	$0.00	$0.00	$0.00	$7143.51	$7143.51

FIXED EXPENDITURES

Add Fixed Description

Fixed Description	Jan	Feb	Mar	Apr	May	Jun	Jan-Jun Total	July	Aug	Sep	Oct	Nov	Dec	July-Dec Total	Total
Mortagage	$ 0.00	$ 0.00	$ 0.00	$ 0.00	$ 0.00	$ 0.00	$ 0.00	$ 900.00	$ 949.88	$ 0.00	$ 0.00	$ 0.00	$ 0.00	$ 1849.88	$ 1849.88
Homeowners Association Fee	$ 0.00	$ 0.00	$ 0.00	$ 0.00	$ 0.00	$ 0.00	$ 0.00	$ 75.94	$ 78.76	$ 0.00	$ 0.00	$ 0.00	$ 0.00	$ 154.70	$ 154.70
Insurance	$ 0.00	$ 0.00	$ 0.00	$ 0.00	$ 0.00	$ 0.00	$ 0.00	$ 117.27	$ 0.00	$ 0.00	$ 0.00	$ 0.00	$ 0.00	$ 117.27	$ 117.27
Auto Payment	$ 0.00	$ 0.00	$ 0.00	$ 0.00	$ 0.00	$ 0.00	$ 0.00	$ 445.99	$ 445.88	$ 0.00	$ 0.00	$ 0.00	$ 0.00	$ 891.87	$ 891.87
Tithes/Charity	$ 0.00	$ 0.00	$ 0.00	$ 0.00	$ 0.00	$ 0.00	$ 0.00	$ 482.00	$ 0.00	$ 0.00	$ 0.00	$ 0.00	$ 0.00	$ 482.00	$ 482.00
Legal	$ 0.00	$ 0.00	$ 0.00	$ 0.00	$ 0.00	$ 0.00	$ 0.00	$ 0.00	$ 0.00	$ 0.00	$ 0.00	$ 0.00	$ 0.00	$ 0.00	$ 0.00

The worksheet above guides you through the three phases of budgeting successfully and will help free up money that you didn't even know you had! For this chapter, I will explain the layout and the operation of the worksheet, the philosophy behind it, and how it will help you overcome any issues or conflicts you may have had before.

The most important goal of budgeting is to ensure that our income is higher than our expenses.

Projected Budget

The first phase of budgeting comes under the category of projected budgeting. In simple terms, this is the look-ahead portion of how we are planning to invest or spend our money. This is the phase of budgeting that most people are familiar with, even if they are not actually practicing it. Using the month as the measure of time, people sit down, together if they are a couple, and hash out what they consider to be the income and the expenses for the upcoming month. Chart #2 below pinpoints the section where we display the sources of projected income and the amounts that are expected from the sources for the month. It also shows the section that all the projected expenses are listed along with the percentages that the expenses are relative to the total projected income given. These expenses can include the mortgage or rental payment, car notes, insurance payments, groceries, cell phone bill, fuel expenses, etc.

The point here is that we gain a greater perspective on how our expenses for the month compared to the income that is anticipated that month. One keynote to add here is the most important goal to budgeting is to ensure that our income is greater than our expenses. This is called living within your means. Too many people from month to month constantly live outside of their means. In other words, their debt/asset ratio continues to increase with each month passing. No long-term financial reward can be obtained with this style of living. Second, if our expenses are greater than our income, then there is no way to begin the process of saving and investing. This keynote is very important to uphold. We have laid out all our expenses, identified how much needs to be allocated to each item, and verified that the expenses total to less than or equal to the income projected. Finally, we have every intention to follow the laid-out plan to the tee. This is the projected budget.

Chart #2: Projected Income & Projected Expenses

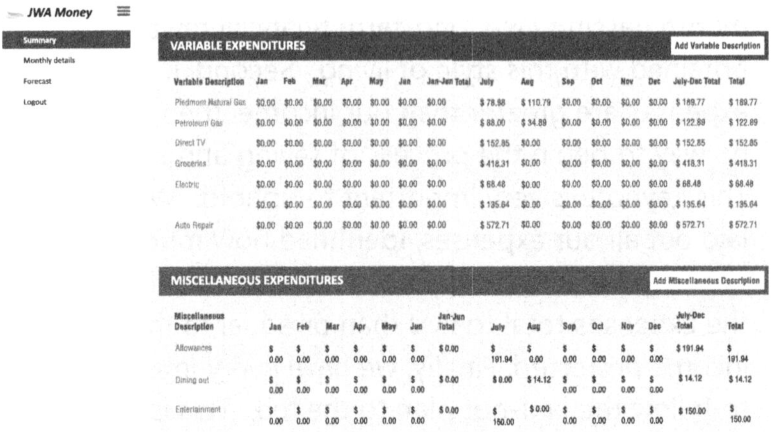

Variable Description	Jan	Feb	Mar	Apr	May	Jun	Jan-Jun Total	July	Aug	Sep	Oct	Nov	Dec	July-Dec Total	Total
Piedmont Natural Gas	$0.00	$0.00	$0.00	$0.00	$0.00	$0.00	$0.00	$ 78.98	$ 110.79	$0.00	$0.00	$0.00	$0.00	$ 189.77	$ 189.77
Petroleum Gas	$0.00	$0.00	$0.00	$0.00	$0.00	$0.00	$0.00	$ 88.00	$ 34.89	$0.00	$0.00	$0.00	$0.00	$ 122.89	$ 122.89
Direct TV	$0.00	$0.00	$0.00	$0.00	$0.00	$0.00	$0.00	$ 152.85	$0.00	$0.00	$0.00	$0.00	$0.00	$ 152.85	$ 152.85
Groceries	$0.00	$0.00	$0.00	$0.00	$0.00	$0.00	$0.00	$ 418.31	$0.00	$0.00	$0.00	$0.00	$0.00	$ 418.31	$ 418.31
Electric	$0.00	$0.00	$0.00	$0.00	$0.00	$0.00	$0.00	$ 68.48	$0.00	$0.00	$0.00	$0.00	$0.00	$ 68.48	$ 68.48
	$0.00	$0.00	$0.00	$0.00	$0.00	$0.00	$0.00	$ 135.64	$0.00	$0.00	$0.00	$0.00	$0.00	$ 135.64	$ 135.64
Auto Repair	$0.00	$0.00	$0.00	$0.00	$0.00	$0.00	$0.00	$ 572.71	$0.00	$0.00	$0.00	$0.00	$0.00	$ 572.71	$ 572.71

Miscellaneous Description	Jan	Feb	Mar	Apr	May	Jun	Jan-Jun Total	July	Aug	Sep	Oct	Nov	Dec	July-Dec Total	Total
Allowances	$ 0.00	$ 0.00	$ 0.00	$ 0.00	$ 0.00	$ 0.00	$ 0.00	$ 191.94	$ 0.00	$ 0.00	$ 0.00	$ 0.00	$ 0.00	$ 191.94	$ 191.94
Dining out	$ 0.00	$ 0.00	$ 0.00	$ 0.00	$ 0.00	$ 0.00	$ 0.00	$ 0.00	$ 14.12	$ 0.00	$ 0.00	$ 0.00	$ 0.00	$ 14.12	$ 14.12
Entertainment	$ 0.00	$ 0.00	$ 0.00	$ 0.00	$ 0.00	$ 0.00	$ 0.00	$ 150.00	$ 0.00	$ 0.00	$ 0.00	$ 0.00	$ 0.00	$ 150.00	$ 150.00

Actual Budget

This is the point where most budgeting strategies have their ending point. Everyone has prepared a very compelling budget sheet that has compensated for every possible expense for the upcoming month, and then the month takes place. And the first week of the month, the budget is blown! Whether it is because emergency maintenance is needed on the car or the iPhone was dropped in the toilet, it does not matter. Everyone becomes frustrated because they did not see the iPhone falling out of the back pocket into the pool of the abyss. What they fail to realize is that their budgeting process has not failed them in that moment of emergency. They must take it into phase two: The Actual Budget. This budgeting phase requires tracking of the expenses as they happen in conjunction with the income as it is actually paid. For instance, the mortgage is usually due on the 1st of the month with a grace period until the 5th. However, if our paycheck comes bimonthly, then our sign of income may not appear until the 15th of the month. In most cases, people have planned it ahead enough so that even though the mortgage must be paid before the income is paid, they have enough in their bank account to hold over until the income is received.

Chart #3: Actual Income & Actual Expenses

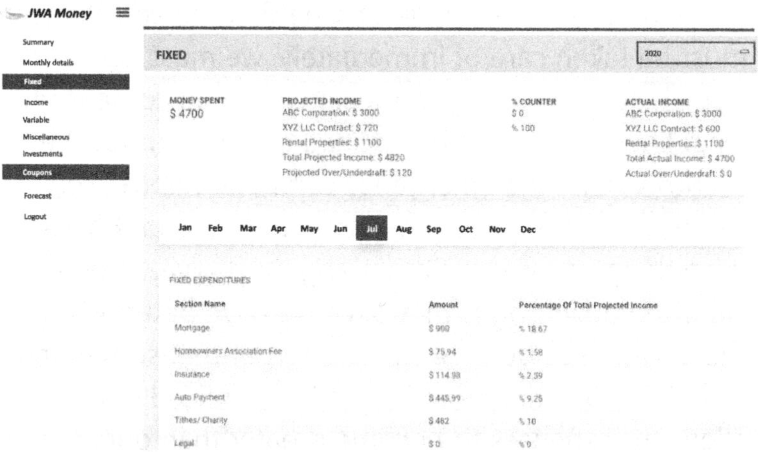

But what about the iPhone replacement? Our business is dependent on having that phone operational. We can't afford to wait until the 15th when the income comes in. How do we get past this point? Plus, an iPhone replacement was not included in the Projected Budget. How can we compensate for that? This is where the Actual Budget lines are so important. As expenses come in each line item, we now have the responsibility to determine how much money is left in each category. Chart #3 shows the area of the budget sheet that keeps track of the amount of projected income that was collected and deposited into the banking account along with what is remaining of each category amount that was given in the projected expenses.

If an emergency expense occurs, we must determine how much of an emergency it really is. Does the expense have to be taken care of immediately? Or is it such that we can delay it until the next projected budgeting cycle? If we determine that the emergency must be taken care of immediately, we must figure out where in the budget the expenses can come from; what line item can be postponed or canceled for the month so that the emergency can be covered? You can have anything that you want, but you can't have everything you want. Something must give. Where we often go wrong is that once we have determined the budget has been blown, we forget that something scheduled for that month must be sacrificed unless we allow our expenses to become greater than our income. Some people can budget a category such as miscellaneous expenses, which serves like an overhead line item in the budget that accounts for things not identified during the projected budgeting phase. This could then serve to fund the emergency expense that has just occurred.

You can have anything that you want, but you can't have everything you want.

As the month continues, the Actual Budget continually reveals what the remaining balances are for each line item in the sheet so that if any additional expenses occur that were not accounted for, we are able to figure out a plan on how to compensate for them. Finally, the Actual Budget allows us to see if the amounts that we allocated to each projected line item were accurate amounts. It will tell us if we spent more than was projected. If we overspend, then the task at hand is to see what line item we can underspend to offset the overall expenditure. As an example, there was a month that my grocery bill was overspent by $125, which is significant. However, I was anticipating having an insurance co-payment of $200 for a previous car accident that was being settled. It turned out that by the end of the month, the car settlement still had not been finalized, so the fact that I did not have to pay the $200 to the insurance company allowed me to compensate that $200 to cover the $125 that I overspent on the grocery.

Summary Budget

I consider this to be the most important phase of budgeting. However, it is the phase that most people do not incorporate into their budgeting process. The Summary Budget is the after-the-fact portion of the process. How did we do during the previous period with our budget? Everyone needs to be able to answer that question in order to make their budgeting an effective one. For the Projected Budget, we sat down and determined what our budget would look like before the month began. In the Actual Budget, we kept track of expenses and income as they occurred and determined what was left in case emergencies popped up and we had to reallocate funding from one-line item to another. For the Summary Budget, we tally up all expense line items as well as determine differentials between projected income and actual income. Now it is time to compare and see where our money was spent. Chart #4 illustrates a sample look of what the summary budget sheet looks like to complete the Budgeting in THREE Dimensions! package. The summary budget sheet is represented on the Master Summary Sheet, while the projected and actual budgets are tracked on the monthly budget sheets.

Chart #4: Summary Budget Sheet

JWA Money

- Summary
- Monthly details
- Forecast
- Logout

INCOME — Add Income Description

Income Description	Jan	Feb	Mar	Apr	May	Jun	Jan-Jun Total	July	Aug	Sep	Oct	Nov	Dec	July-Dec Total	Total
ABC Corporation	$0.00	$0.00	$0.00	$0.00	$0.00	$0.00	$0.00	$ 3000.00	$ 3000.00	$0.00	$0.00	$0.00	$0.00	$ 6000.00	$ 6000.00
XYZ LLC Contract	$0.00	$0.00	$0.00	$0.00	$0.00	$0.00	$0.00	$ 600.00	$ 600.00	$0.00	$0.00	$0.00	$0.00	$ 1200.00	$ 1200.00
Rental Properties	$0.00	$0.00	$0.00	$0.00	$0.00	$0.00	$0.00	$ 1100.00	$0.00	$0.00	$0.00	$0.00	$0.00	$ 1100.00	$ 1100.00

INVESTMENTS — Add Investment Description

Investments Description	Jan	Feb	Mar	Apr	May	Jun	Jan-Jun Total	July	Aug	Sep	Oct	Nov	Dec	July-Dec Total	Total
Janus Henderson	$ 0.00	$ 0.00	$ 0.00	$ 0.00	$ 0.00	$ 0.00	$ 0.00	$ 82.00	$ 142.00	$ 0.00	$ 0.00	$ 0.00	$ 0.00	$ 224.00	$ 224.00
Vanguard Securities	$ 0.00	$ 0.00	$ 0.00	$ 0.00	$ 0.00	$ 0.00	$ 0.00	$ 400.00	$ 477.99	$ 0.00	$ 0.00	$ 0.00	$ 0.00	$ 877.99	$ 877.99

Was the amount spent in each line item justified? As a hypothetical example, if we look at the line item for 'Dining Out' and we find that we spent $1000 eating out, ranging from a fabulous Italian feast at Maggiano's to a bucket of chicken prior to the football game. Is that justified? Or could it be that we frankly ate out way too much last month? Either question could be answered as yes or no.

The point is we must take the time to analyze our spending habits and determine if we need to change something in order to become better financial stewards. If my Summary Budget showed that I had spent $1000 dining out, I would immediately say that I needed to cut that expense in half at least for the next month. That would be $500 that I freed up just by reducing the number of times I go out to eat. The

Summary Budget process is where we find money to free up for investing purposes. Maybe we are a Starbucks fanatic that enjoys having a cafe latte two times during the day. Well, each cafe latte costs, with tax, on average $6.50 per trip. If we get one twice a day, that is $13 per day for the cafe lattes. $13 doesn't sound like that much until we start looking at its equivalence long-term. That $13 per day becomes $65 per week, which becomes $260 per month, which becomes $1560 per year! If we were to cut back to where we only paid a visit to Starbucks once a day, we just saved ourselves $780 per year! Never mind how much we would save if we stopped our Starbucks runs every day and substituted it by buying a French Press coffee maker and making our own 100% Kona whole bean coffee from the store! (And that would be approximately $1278 saved per year, in case you were wondering.)

Budgeting in THREE Dimensions is a three-phase process. If we exclude any phase, our budgeting efforts will be marginal at best. We have created a budget sheet that simplifies including the three phases and extracts all the information that we need to make critical financial decisions needed to make our budgeting process very successful. It helps us regulate our spending habits and helps us find new investment capital that we may not have realized was there. It helps us create new strategies that will help us reduce our expenses and invest the difference!

Chapter 5:

The Financial Dream Blueprint

What is money? Why is so much importance placed on money? What does it take to gain a financial breakthrough? Tony Robbins eloquently describes money as "nothing more than a reflection of your capacity to focus, and your ability to add value and receive back." In my view, I believe that money in many aspects will reflect the success you have had in meeting your passions in life. At the same time, making money can appear to be quite a boring process. It also depends on what our perspective is pertaining to money. What some people consider to be a lot of money is only considered pocket change to others. Our value to society will be in direct correlation to how much income we receive. But our ability to focus on investing with respect to time will determine how much money we will actually make. So if we are looking to put together a blueprint of what our financial dream should look like, it is important to know that 78% of our success in life in prosperity is psychology, and 22% of our success in life in prosperity is mechanical.

Let's take a look at straight numbers for a second. What is the difference between being a millionaire and being a billionaire? For most people, being a millionaire is huge to the point it is hard to imagine what being a millionaire actually looks like. So when trying to compare a millionaire to a billionaire, the feel to them is not that big of a difference. But there is a major difference between the two. Look at it from the perspective of time. Chart #5 shows that if we convert one million seconds to days, the amount comes out to 12 days. That seems to be an enormous period of time. However, if you convert one billion seconds to days, the days are so insurmountable that the days have to be converted to years which comes out to 32 years! That's a tremendous difference between one million and one billion. Keep in mind that one billion surpasses 999 million! Finally, one trillion surpasses 999 billion, which in time equals 31,689 years!

We have the power of choice to determine what we are going to do with that dollar. We can either save it, invest it, or spend it.

Chart #5: Difference Between A Million & A Billion

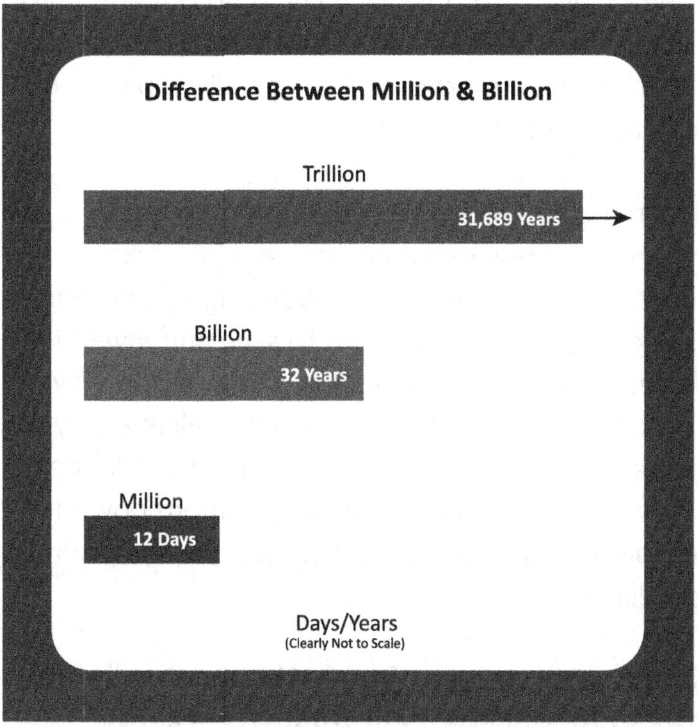

So if we transfer that revelation to dollars, there is a tremendous difference between 12 days' worth of dollars and 32 years' worth of dollars. How do we get from one end to the next? It all comes to that dollar that we currently hold in our pocket- right now! We have the power of choice to determine what we are going to do with that dollar. We can either save it, invest it, or spend it. If we put it into a savings account, that dollar will make us some change in pennies over time. If we invest it, that dollar will make us many dollars for years to come without having to lift a finger. However, if we spend it, that dollar is gone forever, and now we have to go out and make another one. And by all means, don't ever lose that dollar. If you are prone to losing dollars, please go back and reread Chapter 1.

According to Albert Einstein, one of the most ingenious things that a person can do is take advantage of the art of compounding. If you were asking why it is so important to save and invest that dollar, the art of compounding is the reason why. Compounding over time is the most reliable way of increasing your financial wealth. The more money that we are able to accumulate, the more powerful compounding becomes. But what does compounding look like?

Compounding over time is the most reliable way of increasing your financial wealth.

Let's look at it from the standpoint of doubling your dollar. Chart #6 shows that if every year we were able to double the dollars we have saved from the previous year, in Year One, we would have $2.00. In Year Two, we would have $4.00. In Year Three, we would have $8.00. If we were to be disciplined enough to keep our money invested and doubled our money each and every year, by the time we were to get to Year Twenty, our bank account would be holding $1,048,576! That is the art of compounding. But the truth of the matter is very few people have found a way to double the dollar every single year for 20 years. That's a 100% return every year. Unfortunately, when it comes to investing, it doesn't quite work as flawlessly. The first obstacle is the fact that we have to pay taxes. Uncle Sam has to get his share of the wealth. So the amount we have by Year Twenty is in jeopardy of reaching the million-dollar mark. If we were to do the same deal in doubling the dollar except compensating for a 33% tax levy, in Year One, instead of $2.00 saved, we would have only $1.67 saved. In Year Two, we would have only saved $2.79. By the time Year Twenty comes into play, having the exact same discipline to keep our money invested, instead of the $1,048,576 when it was tax-free, we have now only saved $28,463.10! That is a major difference between w/ tax and tax-free. But that is the struggle we have to deal with and why a lot of wealthy people have found ways to decrease their tax obligation.

Chart #6: Doubling the Dollar

Doubling the Dollar with and without Tax

Year	Dollar Double	Dollar Double -33% Tax
1	$2	$1.67
2	$4	$2.79
3	$8	$4.66
4	$16	$7.78
5	$32	$12.99
6	$64	$21.69
7	$128	$36.22
8	$256	$60.49
9	$512	$101.02
10	$1,024	$168.70
11	$2,048	$281.73
12	$4,096	$470.49
13	$8,192	$785.72
14	$16,384	$1,312.15
15	$32,768	$2,191.29
16	$65,536	$3,659.46
17	$131,072	$6,111.29
18	$262,144	$10,205.85
19	$524,288	$17,043.77
20	$1,048,576	$28,463.10

Another example of the differences compounding we can make is as follows. Chart #7 shows two brothers, William and James, pick up on the idea that investing is the best way to use their dollar. However, William picks up on the idea at age 20 and decides to invest $4000 annually for 20 years straight with an annual return of 10%. When William reaches turns age 40, he has accumulated $256,008 thru annual investments and compounding. He decides to stop adding any more money to his investments and allowed the account to sit for the next 25 years.

Chart #7: Brothers Investing and Retiring

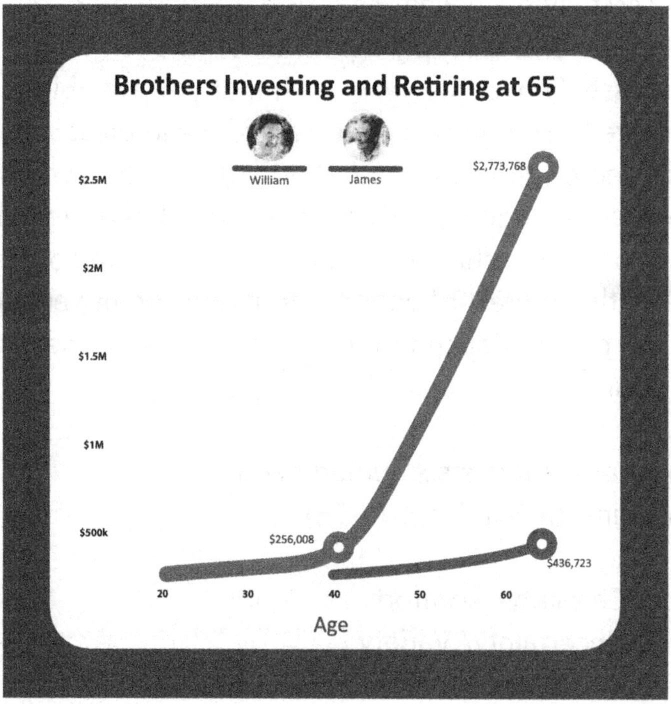

On the other hand, his brother James decides to delay acting on this idea until he turned age 40. At age 40, he decides to invest $4000 annually for the next 25 years, all at an annual return of 10%. When James turns 65 years old, his account ends up with $436,723. However, William's account after turning 65 years old has a total of $2,773,768 for retirement! That is a gap of over $2 million between the two brothers. The moral of this story is the sooner in life we come to the revelation of saving the dollar, the healthier our retirement account will be!

Tony Robbins talks about the six human needs that must be addressed and fulfilled in order to successfully build what he calls a freedom fund. A freedom fund is simply a fund that has been built successfully over the years such that you are able to achieve the six human needs off of the interest received on the account and do not have to work for the income required. That means for all of retirement, your basic monthly expenses and beyond are covered off of the interest of your account and/ or just enough of the principal such that it will cover you for the rest of your life.

So what are those six human needs?
(Robbins, MONEY, pp. 75-78)

1) Certainty/ Comfort
2) Uncertainty/ Variety
3) Significance

4) Love & Connection
5) Growth
6) Contribution

Before we get started on the details, you need to ask yourself these questions:

1) What are you building wealth for?
2) What is it that you are ultimately after?

The answers to these questions will shape our focus on how we will achieve these six human needs. The first need is certainty/ comfort. This allows us to feel like we have some sort of control over our situation and can fairly easily predict what will come next. This is why so many people strive to get their education, find an appropriate career, get married, find the perfect home, have kids, and live life in this format. Most families want the same general things out of life and will fight to receive them. The second need is the opposite of the first need, which is uncertainty/variety. Although the first need is essential, it has the ingredients to become quite boring and put us into a rut which we would want to escape. In the process of going through our predictable patterns in life, we need those surprises and/or problems to show up. We crave the new challenge. We need to have muscle-building competition and resistance to make us become stronger and better than we were before. Although I appreciate my career, it would have been impossible for me to work on the exact same project every day for the duration of it. I needed a change to a new project, a change to a new department, a change to a new company, even a change to a new profession.

The third need is significance. We have a need to feel important in having a very specific purpose. Men have a requirement to feel needed, while women have a requirement to feel wanted. We all want to be perceived as unique and special. This makes us feel powerful and helps exert the best in us by believing we can make a difference to something or someone else. The fourth need is love & connection. We are designed to be in a community with each other as opposed to isolation. Our connections to other people are very important to shaping who we are and our growth. That connection can be a social one through friendships, a physical one through the intimacy of some form, or a spiritual one through prayer and meditation.

The vision of each of the Financial Dream steps has to be made in the mind before there is a chance of achieving that reality.

The last two needs are growth and connection. Growth is an enduring process that, between achievement and resistance to that achievement, we are able to obtain real fulfillment. Everyone needs to experience real fulfillment in their life; otherwise, they are just living as if their spirits were dead. Growth is an introverted need that focuses on the self. However, the contribution is an extroverted need that focuses on others. For contribution, the secret to living is giving and sharing. It all comes together when we know that our efforts and achievement ultimately will be a benefit to others. This brings real fulfillment to ourselves, which causes us to grow and put ourselves in a new position to contribute even more.

Tony Robbins, in his book, also talks about the five financial dreams. They are the following:

1) Financial Security
2) Financial Vitality
3) Financial Independence
4) Financial Freedom
5) Absolute Financial Freedom

(Robbins, MONEY, pp. 214-228)

For our purposes in this book, we will concentrate on what it takes to get to the first step, Financial Security. However, I want you to be aware of what it takes to accomplish all five:

1) Financial Security- the ability to pay for the five basic needs without depending on a paycheck. The five basic needs are rent, food & household, gas & electricity, transportation, and insurance. And let me rephrase what I first said. The

goal is to be able to pay for the five basic needs without ever having to work to pay for them again! That may seem like the goal is far-fetched, but life's costs are less than you may think.

2) Financial Vitality- the ability to pay for the five basic needs plus half of the small indulgences or little luxuries paid without depending on a paycheck.

3) Financial Independence- the pivotal point where the money is now your slave versus you having to slave for the money. A job is no longer necessary to maintain your current lifestyle.

4) Financial Freedom- the ability to pay for everything that you have being financially independent plus 2-3 significant luxuries you want in the future all paid for without having to work.

5) Absolute Financial Freedom- Do anything you want whenever you want! Each step builds upon the previous step until the goal is finally met.

The point here is that the vision of each of the Financial Dream steps has to be made in the mind before there is a chance of achieving that reality. My objective here is to get you geared up to resituate your financial outlook so that Financial Security can become your reality. However, review the previous five financial dreams and determine where your goal should ultimately lie.

Chapter 6:

Getting and Staying Out of Debt

We live in a capitalistic society. You must use your head if you are going to be successful. What is it that you have that everyone else needs that if you could find a way to give it to them, you would be successful? The answer to this question is a blessing and a curse at the same time. Why do I say that? The system is designed so that we can benefit by helping other people gain the gifts that we have and be compensated for it. It also has a loophole designed to find a way to take people's money. In other words, in a capitalistic society, everybody is out to take everyone else's money.

Being in debt, particularly bad debt, is the sloppiest way to allow other people to take your money.

We must be vigilant to make sure that we protect our own money. Money is very slippery and can be lost in an instant. That is why getting out and staying out of debt is so important. Debt is defined as, "a liability or obligation to pay or render something." A loan liability can potentially be good debt or a bad debt. A good loan liability can make a return on its investment or can potentially satisfy a need. A bad loan liability inevitably attracts even more debt without any chance of a return on investment. Being in debt, particularly bad debt, is the sloppiest way to allow other people to take your money. Finance charges, late fees, even speeding tickets are insane ways to just hand over money to someone else, whether it is a credit card company, a small business or, the government. Never mind the illegal ways demonstrated in Chapter 1. (By the way, I got word that the people behind the IRS scam I described have been caught and are currently awaiting their justice; however, not before they had taken people for over 16 million dollars in hard-earned money.)

If you find that you have been a victim of handing money over to these types of capitalist opportunists, then you have picked up the right book and are on course reading this far. We must start by defining what the means to the end is for you financially. Money is a means to an end. However, if you don't define how that end serves others, the money will not come. So, we must come up with a way to serve others and set our financial cycle up so that we have our money working for us instead of us working for the money. How do we go about this?

We must determine what our financial goals are. Are we saving for retirement, to purchase a new home, to send our kids to college, or all the above? These need to be divided into long-term and short-term goals. Are these goals that we plan to execute in 2-5 years, 5-10 years, or 10+ years? How feasible and realistic are these goals when combined to execute them all within their respective time periods? Once we can answer these questions, we can create the discipline in our spending by writing out a financial spending plan that properly encompasses these goals.

We combine the short/long-term financial spending plan with the use of the Budgeting in THREE Dimensions spreadsheet, and we will be able to maximize the use of our money. Our self-wealth will increase as it correlates with how we give of ourselves to others which, in turn, correlates to how well we handle our money. But all of this starts with creating a strategy to get out of bad debt and become debt-free.

Money is very slippery and can be lost in an instant.

What are the biggest contributors to our bad debt? The three contributors are taxes, fees, and interest. According to Chart #8, the bigger chunk of lifetime earnings paying something else besides our personal lifestyles is due to taxes and fees. A whopping 54.4% of gross income is paid in some form of taxes by the average American in a lifetime. Another 15.7% of gross income is paid in interest fees by the average American in a lifetime. So, we need to look in further detail, particularly on where this 54.4% is coming from and what we can do to effectively reduce our tax burden. This leaves a measly 29.9% of gross income!

That's all that is left for the average American to pay for their lifestyle and build their critical mass for financial freedom. So, being purposeful in our financial planning will help us reduce that tax amount and pay Uncle Sam no more than what he is duly owed.

Chart #8: The Golden Egg

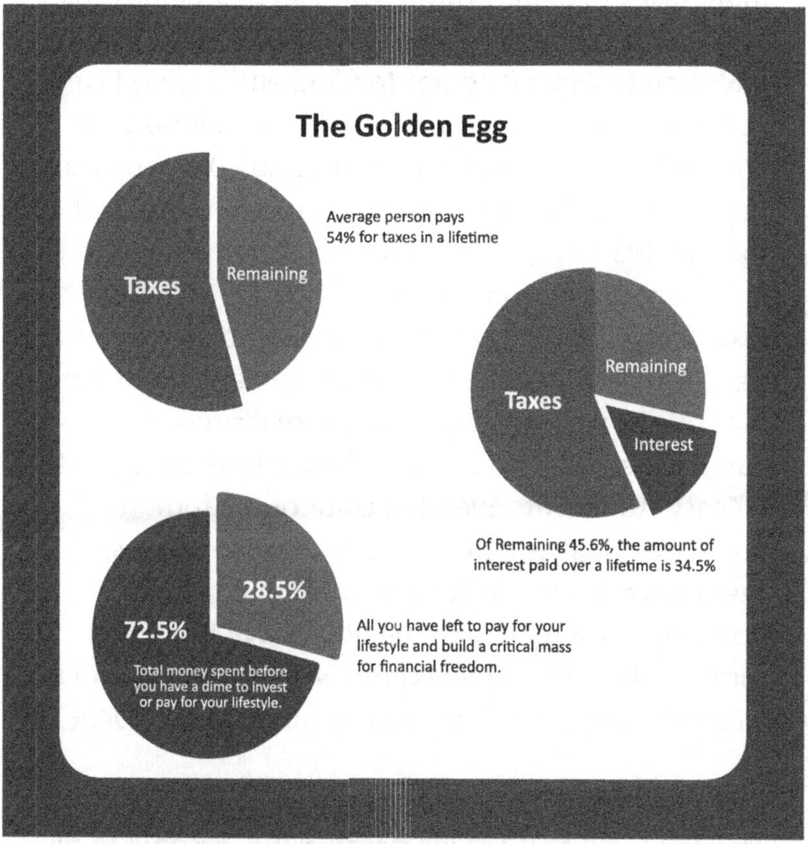

(Robbins, MONEY, pp. 277)

Let's first talk about taxes. Unfortunately, we are unable to get away from paying taxes. However, we can put financial strategies in place that will help reduce our tax burden. April 15th! Everybody recognizes that date as the national day when income taxes are due. Shame on Uncle Sam for having the audacity to dip into our paychecks! There is a shocking statistic that over 84% of Americans pay more taxes than they owe! How can that be possible? Two things come to mind of which we should pay attention to when it comes to filing and paying taxes. For federal taxes, anyone who is filing their taxes on Form 1040EZ is probably paying up to 40% above and beyond what they are required to pay in taxes. Notice that the IRS does not send out tax statements giving a finite amount of what we owe. They are willing to take as much money as we are willing to give them. Because many people have no understanding of the tax code or want to avoid it because it's too complicated, they fill out the 1040EZ form because it is "easy" to fill out. Even the color of the form (the green one) makes it attractive to fill out. However, there is a price to pay for easy, and that price is donating extra money to the IRS. Leave the green form on the table. Even Form 1040A (the red form) is a donation to the IRS, but not as much as the 1040EZ.

Our goal should be to gain all the deductions and credits on our taxes as we deserve. So, prepare to fill out Form 1040 to gain maximum tax deductions. But we must become more informed as to what type of things are tax deductible. As an example, if someone has a job that requires them to drive their car to various locations throughout the course of the day, the miles they put on their car for business purposes are tax deductible. However, they must log those miles and separate them from the miles on the car for personal use. For them to take advantage of those miles, they need to know that information before the year starts and prepare their log accordingly so that at the end of the year, they can take advantage of those deductions. I recommend using software like Turbo Tax to file taxes because Turbo Tax takes you through every deduction that may apply to you. That way, even if you did not prepare accordingly to take the deduction, you can take the measures to take the deduction the following year. As an example, my family had a year that we owed Uncle Sam a total of $66 for the entire year! No, not a tax refund of $66; we only paid Uncle Sam $66! Although I haven't had another year that low, by taking all the deductions for our home office expenses for our home daycare, our tax obligations were reduced that much. That is a Segway to the next aha moment regarding taxes.

If we work or have worked as an employee for a company or small business, at the end of the year, we receive a statement from the company called Form W-2. That form tells us how much earnings we received from the company for the previous year and the state and federal taxes that were paid out of the earnings before we received a dime. This is what I need to alert you to. As an employee, there is an order to which we receive our money. First comes the gross earnings that we made according to our employment contract with the company. Second, the taxes that we owe according to a percentage of our gross earnings are immediately taken out of our check. That is a portion of the 54.4% that we talked about previously. What is left over is given to us in net earnings that will be used to pay whatever expenses we have. In part, that is the 34.5% that we referred to in the previous chart as part of the interest and fees. Once those expenses are paid, whatever is left over is what we must create our lifestyle with. Doesn't sound like much is left over. Having a W-2 form puts you in this pecking order:

1. Gross Earnings
2. Taxes Deducted
3. **Expenses**
4. You

Now, what if you were running your own business? Instead of being an employee, you became a consultant in the same job or left the company and started your own small business. What would change as far as the pecking order is concerned? Well, the change is tremendous. Instead of receiving a W-2 form as an employee, you are now an S-corporation or a limited liability company that receives a Form 1099 for the same work. The pecking order is now as follows:

1. Gross Earnings
2. **Expenses**
3. Taxes Deducted
4. You

Why is the switch of the middle pecking order so important? Recall that as an employee, the taxes deducted are a certain percentage of the gross earnings depending on what tax bracket you belong to. Nevertheless, the percentage comes from the "gross" earned. As a business owner, expenses come "before" taxes are deducted. So as an example, if you have a home office that represents 25% of the square footage of the home, part of your expenses become 25% of your mortgage, the electricity bill, water bill, natural gas bill, and any other expense associated with your house for the year, 25% of that becomes a business expense that is deducted from your gross earnings! Because of the switch, the amount that is considered taxable income is greatly reduced from what was considered gross income! If you have a business that requires a vehicle or vehicles to operate, the payments for the vehicle(s) are a part of those expenses. The reason that I only paid $66 for that one year is that all the expenses to get the home daycare up and running were deducted from our income to the point that the only taxable income that was left over only levied us paying $66. So, becoming an independent contractor vs. an employee can greatly reduce your tax obligation.

In my opinion, paying interest charges is the same as taking a "Big Headed" Ben Franklin 100-dollar bill and setting it ablaze in a campfire!

Now let's focus on interest and fees. Referring to the chart, of the remaining 45.6% of our earnings left after taxes, the amount of interest paid over a lifetime is 18.1% of our total earnings, and hidden fees consuming an additional approximately 4.2% of our total earnings over a lifetime. That leaves us with a whopping 23.3% left over after taxes, fees, and interest to pay for our lifestyles and build our critical mass for financial freedom. We must focus on the causes of fees and accumulated interest. Where do fees come from? In summary, capitalism allows fees to be everywhere. There are credit card late fees, investment fees, transportation fees, ticket purchase fees, annual fees, and membership fees, just to name a few. None of these fees are related to taxes or operational costs of a product or service. They are just extra fees. For example, Chart #9 shows us what happens if we allow annual investment fees to get out of hand.

Chart #9: Impact of Fees

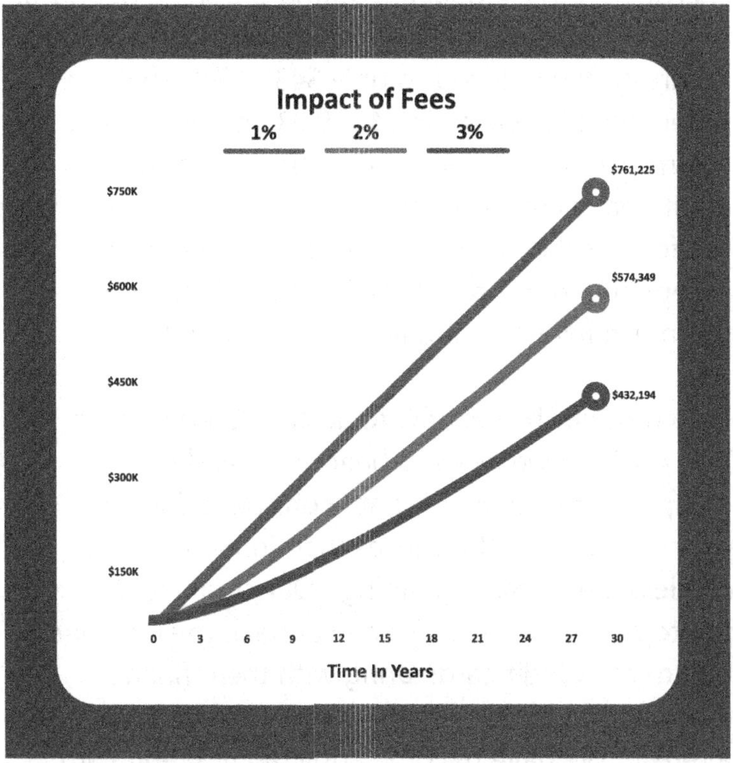

(Robbins, MONEY, pp. 107)

Here, we have an investment of $100,000 for a 30-year period. We will assume that the annualized return on this investment is 8% during that course in time. If the brokerage firm that is handling our account for this term is charging a 1% annual fee for their services, then by the end of the 30 years, our $100,000 investment would have grown to become $761,225!

However, if we allowed that same brokerage firm to charge us a 3% annual fee during the same period of the term, our grand return on our investment would be drastically reduced to only $432,194! That is a difference of a whopping $329,031 of investment returns we were denied simply because of a 2% additional increase in annual fees! For any investment service or other service necessary, we should not accept any more than 1.5% in annual fees! There is too much investment gain at risk if we do!

Let's turn our heads now to accumulated interest. This is where we need to bear down and gain complete control over what I consider a foolish expense. One of the causes mentioned before is reckless credit card spending. Our credit cards are on the top of the list that we must attack to erase our bad debt. Credit cards bring with them finance charges that can range anywhere from 15-22% interest. We have become addicted to credit card spending, buying way more in retail than we have in the bank account, which leads to paying wasteful interest charges. In my opinion, paying interest charges is the same as taking a "Big Headed" Ben Franklin 100-dollar bill and setting it ablaze in a campfire. Let's eliminate this behavior from this point forward.

First, we must access our current financial position. How much credit card debt are we in? To determine this, we must list the credit card companies that have outstanding balances. Then we list them in priority according to which credit cards have the highest interest rate. The highest interest rate is the first credit card that must be paid off in full. Do not try to pay off all the outstanding credit cards at once. Our resources should be focused solely on that card.

This does two things for us. First, it allows us to pay off one card faster by being able to apply more principal to the payment. If we spread out the payments amongst all the outstanding credit cards, then less principal is paid on all the cards, and most of our payments will go to interest only. Second, the remaining credit card accounts will go dormant, and the credit card company will eventually close the account due to lack of activity. Whereas, if we keep paying the minimum payment every month, the account will stay active, we continue to pay only interest payments decreasing the principal down in infinitesimal increments and continue to be in bad debt.

Although they will put a bad credit rating on your credit report once we stop making the minimum payments, this is not the time to worry about that; our credit is already bad. This works to our advantage, for once we finally pay off the first credit card to a zero balance, we will be in a position to negotiate a fair price with the credit card company. This buys off the bad credit rating from our record, which could be only paying 50% of the credit principal over a predetermined period. From the credit card company's viewpoint, when they close an account due to inactivity, they write off the account and its balance as a loss. A year or two later, when you contact them about buying off the account, any money they collect relative to your account is considered additional assets, so they are eager to come to an agreement within a six-month period or so. That is why negotiation of 50% of the amount owed is a very viable option. We continue this strategy until we can pay off the last of the principal on all our credit card debt.

Now that we have accomplished that major milestone, we need to analyze the remaining debt that we have, which should be classified as good debt. This should include mortgage payments, car notes, and other payments for rental properties, real estate, etc. At the same time, we should notice that some monies have been freed up since we have eliminated the bad debt. Remember that monies and interest that have been saved due to the credit card and loans being paid in full should be invested. Now that we have created a sound discipline to reduce our debt, we have also created a discipline to reduce our expenses as we are no longer spending above our means.

Rule of thumb, we must maximize our good debt to continue to reduce our expenses and invest the difference. Note how amazing it is that so much capital has freed up just because you have made it to this point. Now the remaining debt that we have has to be considered based on its interest. Our goal is to pay off the mortgage and the car notes in accordance with beating the associated interest rate. In other words, if we have a timeshare payment that is associated with a 12% interest rate being the highest debt rate we have left, then we become aggressive with it by adding a "principal only" payment so that we can accelerate the payoff faster.

However, if we have a mortgage that is running a 6% interest rate and the associated interest rate with investments is running at 8.5%, then our strategy would be to pay the mortgage payment according to the amount owed and use what would have been the principal only payment to invest. We make much better use of our money investing in an 8.5% rate of return versus paying off a 6% interest rate as a 2.5% interest difference can get us to our financial goals a lot faster. The gamble is that the investment may not make above the 6% interest rate for the year. Nevertheless, the emphasis is to feed the discipline of investing regardless of the situation at hand. It is a muscle that needs to be strengthened over time.

(Table #1) demonstrates the power that the 2.5% interest difference can have on building our financial capital. A mere $5 per day investment can have a tremendous effect on our wealth building in just a 20-year period. If we received a 10% annual rate of return, $5 each day would amount to $113,905 in 20 years! Get excited about finding that $5 to invest!

So, now that we have put all the emphasis on getting rid of bad debt, what differentiates bad debt from good debt? Well, good debt comes in the form of a loan to start up a business or a mortgage from the purchase of a house or a condominium. It can also come in the form of a basic need such as a car loan. Usually, this type of debt is an agreement with a bank, mortgage company, or a loaning institution. The terms of repayment come in the form of an amortization schedule. An amortization schedule is a prearrangement between the loaning institution and the customer of when payments will be due over the course of the loan period and what portions of the payments go towards the principal balance, and what portions go towards accruing interests. The loan period can cover anywhere from a 5-year loan all the way up to a 30-year loan.

Table #1: Early Start Nest Egg

Early Start Nest Egg

(Assumes 10% Annual Rate of Return)

Daily Inv.	Month Inv.	10 years	20 years	30 years	40 years	50 years
$5	$150	30,727	113,905	339,073	948,612	2,598,659
$10	$300	61,453	227,811	678,146	1,897,224	5,197,317
$15	$450	92,180	341,716	1,017,220	2,845,836	7,795,976
$20	$600	122,907	455,621	1,356,293	3,794,448	10,394,634
$30	$900	184,360	683,432	2,034,439	5,691,672	15,591,952
$40	$1,200	245,814	911,243	2,712,586	7,588,895	20,789,269
$50	$1,500	307,267	3,390,732	3,390,732	9,486,119	25,986,586

(Robbins, MONEY, pp. 259)

(Assumes 10% Annual Rate of Return)

The interest rate is also declared prior to the agreement, which is normally based on some mathematical formula relative to the prime rate declared by the Federal Bank. The rate will either be a fixed rate, which means that the same rate will apply throughout the course of the loan, or the interest will be on an adjustable rate mortgage (ARM), which means the rate may fluctuate based on the varying change of the Federal interest rates. When the loaning institution offers the fixed rate versus the ARM, the ARM will have the lower rate attached to it. However, the gamble is that the ARM may possibly rise higher than the fixed rate as the loan period progresses, which means the customer will end up paying more interest over the course of the loan if the federal rates increase.

An amortization schedule is a pre-arrangement between the loaning institution and the customer of when payments will be due over the course of the loan period and what portions of the payments go towards the principal balance, and what portions go toward accruing interests.

So how does the amortization schedule work? Well, let's look at an example. If we have a 30-year fixed-rate loan at 6% interest of a $270,000 mortgage, the loaning institution will calculate what the monthly payments will be for the course of the loan. In this case, the monthly payment is $1618.79.

Table #2: U.S. Home Amortization Schedule

US Home Amortization Schedule

Month	Payment	Principal	Interest	Balance
Jan	$1618.79	$268.79	$1350.00	$269,731.21
Feb	$1618.79	$270.13	$1348.66	$269,461.08
Mar	$1618.79	$271.48	$1347.31	$269,189.60
Apr	$1618.79	$272.84	$1345.95	$268,916.76

(Robbins, MONEY, pp. 254)

Note: - Average cost of an American home: $270,000
- 30-year Fixed-Rate Loan @ 6% Interest
- Benefits of "For Principal Only" or Pocket Change Prepayments

Now the average person may think that when paying this amount of money, half will go to paying off the principal, and half will go to interest. Not a chance. The purpose of the amortization schedule is so that the loaning institution can get most of its profit on the front end of the loan.

In other words, if it worked according to the average loan for the payment mentioned previously, $809.40 would go to paying off the principal. According to (Table #2), only $268.79 is paid toward the principal on the 1st payment. That means $1350.00 is paid towards interest on the very 1st payment. The higher the interest rate on loan, the lower the principal portion will be on the first payment.

If the interest rate was higher, the amount going to principal would be even less. The most that would be paid to the principal during the loan would be the last payment, which, in this case, would be Payment #60.

The higher the interest rate on the loan, the lower the principal portion will be on the first payment.

Chart #8 shows that if the same terms mentioned above were for a $1,000,000 home mortgage, by the time you reached Payment #60, you would have paid $2,160,000 in total payments, which translates into $1,160,000 in interest only! That's a lot of money to be paying other people! And this is classified as good debt. How can we possibly combat this? Is there any way to cut our costs with this amortization concept?

If we were to continue applying these principal-only payments, our pay-it-forward strategy would pay off the 30- year mortgage in approximately 15 years!

There is. I consider this the effect of "principal only" payments. Principal only payments is an added payment in addition to the normal mortgage payments, which are applied only to pay down the principal.

Chart #10: Mortgage Interest Payments

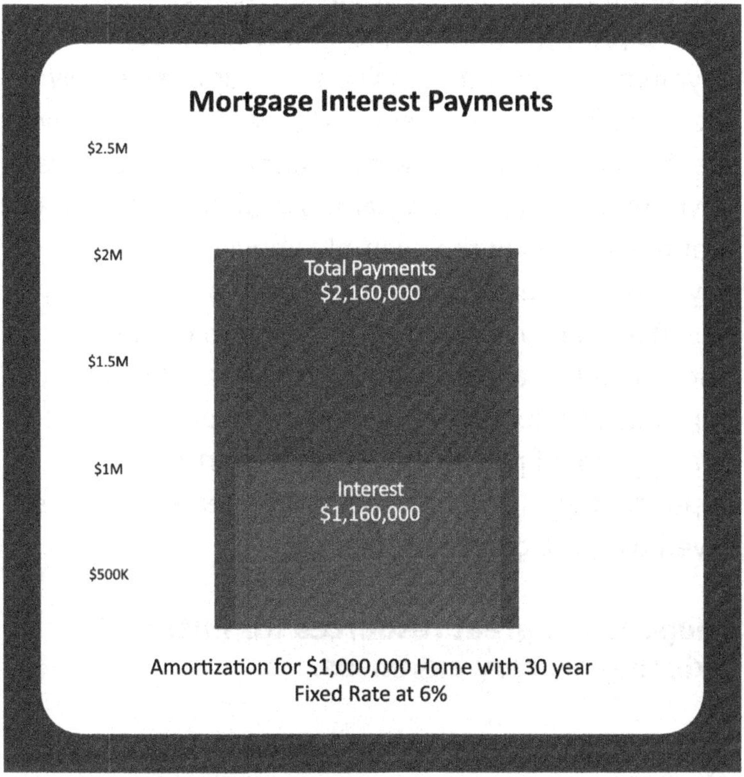

(Robbins, MONEY, pp. 252)

Notes:

1) At 6% interest, 80% of your mortgage payment will go towards interest.
2) Interest payments will tack on an additional 100% or more to your loan value.
3) Prepay your next month's "For Principal Only" could pay off a 30-year mortgage in 15 years or so.

If our initial payment is $1618, we can add an additional $270 for principal only. Principal only is an amount that you will never pay interest on. If we make a principal only on the 1st payment, our next payment becomes the equivalent to approximately the 3rd payment. In other words, we literally skip over the 2nd payment on the amortization schedule. This payment includes a heavy amount of interest payment that is avoided. In the example above, the 2nd payment of interest would have been a total of $1348.66 that was saved by applying that one principal only payment. If we were to continue applying principal only payments, our pay-it-forward strategy would pay off the 30-year mortgage in approximately 15 years! That is 15+ years of interest saved over the course of the loan.

Coupons are great resources for further reducing grocery expenses.

Now that we have a grasp of how to overcome bad debt and effectively manage good debt, what other means can we use to breakdown our debt, reduce expenses, and invest the difference? We must change our financial habits if we are going to get different financial results. It is the small things that, once addressed, make big differences. For example, do you make a shopping list before you go to the grocery store? This one gesture is crucial to minimizing duplicate purchases. I remember playing hide and seek at a friend's house, hiding in their kitchen pantry.

I noticed that they had 5 unopened boxes of aluminum foil sitting on one of the shelves. I remember saying to myself, who needs five boxes of aluminum foil. Then to my dismay, his mother came home that day with another box of aluminum foil in the grocery bag making six boxes total. Making a grocery list keeps us informed of the inventory of food we already have at the house so that we can pay the grocery store the minimal amount possible without investing in excess products that, because of our inventory, may not open for another 6 months. Next, I love to substitute paper for money. That means cutting coupons. Coupons are great resources for further reducing grocery expenses.

Take your leftovers to work for lunch instead of eating out.

I made it a habit to cut coupons out of the Sunday newspaper while watching football games (it also gave me the excuse I needed to actually sit down in front of the TV to watch the game without having to be interrupted with the "Honey-Do" list). Most of my shopping was based on being able to use the coupons I cut. As an example, for a whole year in keeping track of coupons used, I had saved a total of $687.95! Now that is $687.95 that was paid in paper instead of Big-Headed Ben Franklins! And clearly, coupon cutting is a great strategy to reduce household expenses and invest the difference. Now that we have bought grocery at a reduced cost and have cooked the food from the grocery store, usually, all the food cooked is not consumed at the first table sitting. There are usually leftovers after the food is prepared. Here comes the next strategy that will reduce expenses.

Take your leftovers to work for lunch instead of eating out. This helps reduce expenses on two fronts. First, a typical lunch out at work will cost around $8 per day. If you are eating out every day at work, that's 5 days in consideration which amounts to $40 per week. If we translate that on a grander scale, that converts to $160 per month or approximately $1920 per year. Now my daughter likes to refer to me as the father, Julius, from the TV show, "Everybody Hates Chris," where he will calculate the cost lost from the spilled milk on the counter (which is approximately $0.42 worth). I take pride with that label when it comes to discussing money management. We are eating out for lunch every day at work while cooking in abundance at home so that leftovers are constantly produced. That means not only are we spending $1920 each year on lunches, but we are also throwing away leftovers that have spoiled in the back of the refrigerator. So what? In a typical home of a family of four people, the average cost of food thrown away in a typical kitchen after cooking a meal is approximately $145 each month. That translates into throwing away $1740 worth of food each year! Combine that with the money spent on work lunches, the total is $3660 that can be freed up if we were only to take our leftovers to work for lunch.

Now by no means am I saying to never each out again at work. Going out to eat one time each week will still allow you to eat all the leftovers so that none of them go to waste and will still free up a lot of capital and invest the difference. And it is not just limited to lunch. Purchasing cafe lattes on the way to work every day also consumes a lot of capital. The average cost of a cafe latte is $6.50 per trip. Often people end up going for a cafe latte twice a day. Those two trips a day will cost $260 over the course of a month or $1560 over the course of a year. So does the math for the person who makes two cafe latte trips, goes out to eat every day for work, and throws away all those leftovers at their house! There is too much at stake to have investment capital going down the drain.

Chapter 7:

The Art and the Importance of Compounding Interest

Albert Einstein stated, "Compound interest is the greatest mathematical discovery of all time. "Compound interest is the oldest and most reliable form of generating wealth. However, most people fail to make this form of generating wealth a part of their lifestyle because either they are unaware of the concept or it does not generate wealth quickly enough for them. Everyone is looking for the get-rich-quick scheme, all the while wasting time that could have been used to get compound interest working on their behalf. The only things that are needed to generate wealth are discipline, motivation, consistency, and time. Compound interest can be defined as the occurrence of interest on a financial account that accrues to an amount of money that in turn accrues interest itself.

The only things that are needed to generate wealth are discipline, motivation, consistency, and time.

Although time is necessary for this to reach its potential, compound interest is an extremely powerful tool in creating wealth. How much time does it take?

That's a good question. Let's look at it from the standpoint of doubling the dollar. As we had stated before, once you receive a dollar, you can either save it and let it work for you or spend it, which is the end of that dollar. Let's say we decide to save that dollar and every dollar we get as a result of it. After the first year, that dollar doubles, so now we have $2. We reinvest those dollars, and in the second year, those dollars double to where we now have $4. If we were to continue the trend of doubling the dollar by year 20, we would have over $1 million in our account. Unfortunately, there are major nemeses to the doubling the dollar scheme, and they are taxes!

As we stated in Chapter 5, there is a major difference in the amount saved in a pure doubling of the dollar in 20 years versus doubling the dollar minus a 33% tax deduction. If you add that to the fact a typical savings account will only give you a 1-2% interest rate of return versus a 100% rate of return, it becomes even more paramount that we become very disciplined when it comes to investing and investing wisely.

With the tax deduction, in 20 years, we will only have a little over $28,000 in our account! That is a long way from $1 million. But the sooner we realize it is imperative that we start saving and investing, the better off we will be at retirement.

More time upfront to compound interest with less money will result in more overall than

investing more money with less time to compound interest.

A person who starts a savings account at the age of 25 investing $500 per month at 7% interest for the next 30 years will end up with more money than a person who starts a savings account at the age of 35 investing $1500 per month at 7% interest for the next 20 years. This also goes for a person who invests $1000 annually from the time between ages 25-35 years. They will end up with more money if they invest only between 25-35 years and never invest another dime, but lets it sit thru 65 years versus a person who invests $1000 annually starting at 35 years all the way through 65 years.

In Chart #11, Susan invests $5000 annually between the ages of 25-35 for a total investment of $50,000. By the time she reaches 65 years of age, she has a total of <u>$602,070</u> in her account. On the other hand, Bill invests $5000 annually between the ages 35-65, 10 years later than Susan but 20 years longer than Susan. Bill's total investment is $150,000 versus $50,000 invested by Susan, yet, by the time Bill reaches 65 years of age, he only has a total of <u>$540,741</u>. So, more time upfront to compound interest with less money will result in more overall than investing more money with less time to compound interest.

But, do not forget in the chart where Chris invested $5000 annually the whole period from age 25-65 for a total investment of $200,000; his overall amount at age 65 is $1,142,811!!

Chart #11: Growth of Savings Accounts

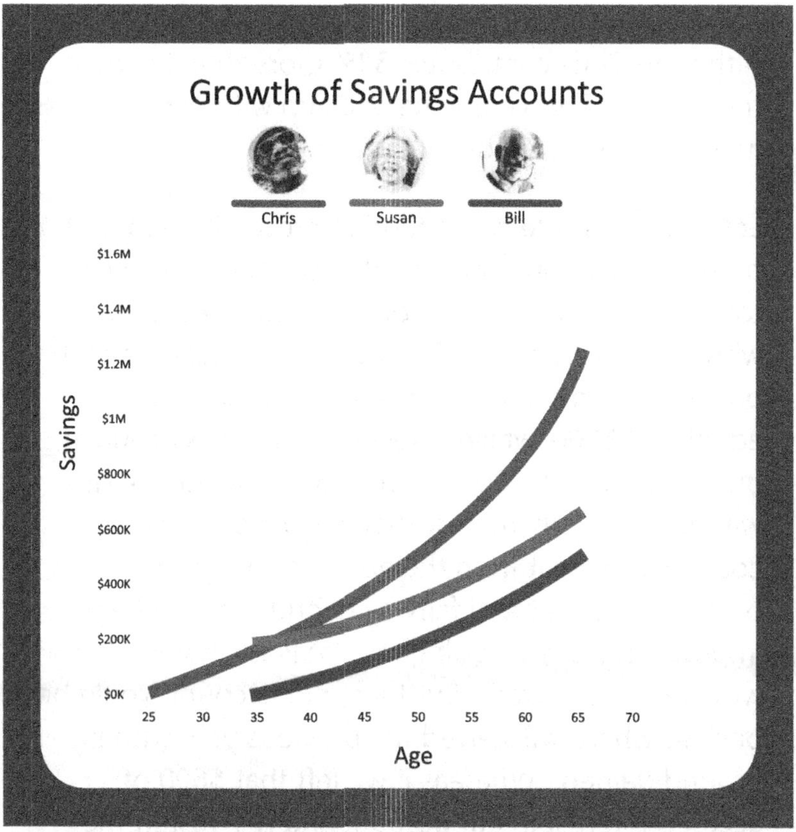

<u>Notes:</u>

1) Susan invests $5000 annually between ages 25 & 35. Total invested: $50,000
2) Bill invests $5000 annually between ages 35 & 65. Total invested: $150,000

3) Chris invests $5000 annually between ages 25 & 65. Total invested: $200,000

Saving Fundamentals: Harnessing the power of compounding can greatly impact the amount of savings over the long term.

Although Chris contributes 33% more than Bill over the course of his career, he ends up with over twice as much wealth as Bill by the age of 65.

Let's demonstrate compound interest a little more for better correlation. Let's say that we have saved up a total of $10,000 that we would like to invest today with an interest rate of 6%. What that means is that one year from today, we will have accrued an additional $600, which gives us a total of $10,600 in our account ($10,000 x 1.06). Now, what do we do with that $600 in interest that we just earned? We could withdraw it from the account and go buy a brand-new driver and fairway hybrid that will help improve our overall golf game (at least that is what we would tell ourselves). But then, our account would be back to where we started the previous year with no ground gained. Whereas if we left that $600 of accrued interest in our account and reinvested the interest for another year, now the art of compounding interest can start to take form. Let's say that for the second year, we once again received 6% interest for the year. At the end of the second year, our initial amount of $10,600 now has grown to $11,236 ($10,600 x 1.06). The interest that we received for year two is $636, which is a $36 increase from the interest in year one!

Start investing as early as you can. People who start the journey of gaining compound interest in this manner are the best candidates to become millionaires solely on compound interest!

Our interest received is increasing over the years, it would behoove us to leave the gains in the account. So, by year three, assuming the constant interest rate of 6%, our nest egg grows from $11,236 by year two to $11,910.16 by year three. The earned interest this time is $674.16, which is now $38.16 more than the second year and $74.16 more than the first year! Keep in mind that our interest continues to compound and increase over the years to the point that many people can retire living off the interest only! That is what 30-40 years of compounded interest can do for us. That is why it is so important to start investing as early as we can. People who start the journey of gaining compound interest in this manner are the best candidates to become millionaires solely on compound interest! That means we only tucked away our savings into an account that strictly received its dividends from interest and, in the process, will become a millionaire. But we don't have to start at 17-years-old to accomplish it. However, the amount that we need to save monthly is based on the age when we begin saving.

So, how can we predict how much money we will be able to save within a specified period? How much money will we be able to make if we invest $10,000 for 5 years in an account that accrues 7.5% interest continuously? Well, if you revert to Chart #11, notice that the curve in which Chris' account grows over the 40-year period is an exponential curve. That equation is defined as follows:

$$\mathbf{A = Pe^{rt}}$$

Where A= total amount gained, P= the initial amount invested, e is the exponential number, r= the rate of interest, and t= the amount of time investment accrues in years. So, in this example, the total amount gained A= (10,000) x e(.075)(5), which amounts to <u>$14,550</u> gained after a 5 year period. With this equation, we can predict and plan how our retirement will build before getting started. The alternate to this equation is where your interest compounds either monthly, quarterly, or semiannually. If this is the case, then the equation to calculate how much would accrue is as follows:

$$\mathbf{A = P(1+r/n)^{nt}}$$

Where n= the number of times per year the interest compounds. So if the investment account compounds quarterly, the total amount gained A= (10,000) x (1+(0.075)/ (4))(4)(5) = <u>$14,499</u>. Notice that for continuous interest accrual, the amount gained after 5 years is more with the amount gained for interest accrual on a quarterly basis.

Now that we know how to calculate our savings amount over time, let's get back to discussing how to get to a million dollars for retirement. For this case, let's say that all throughout, we continue to receive a 6% return rate. If we look at Chart #12, it confirms that we need to save a lot less per month to make millionaire status by the time we are age 65.

Chart #12: Saving for a One Million Dollar Retirement

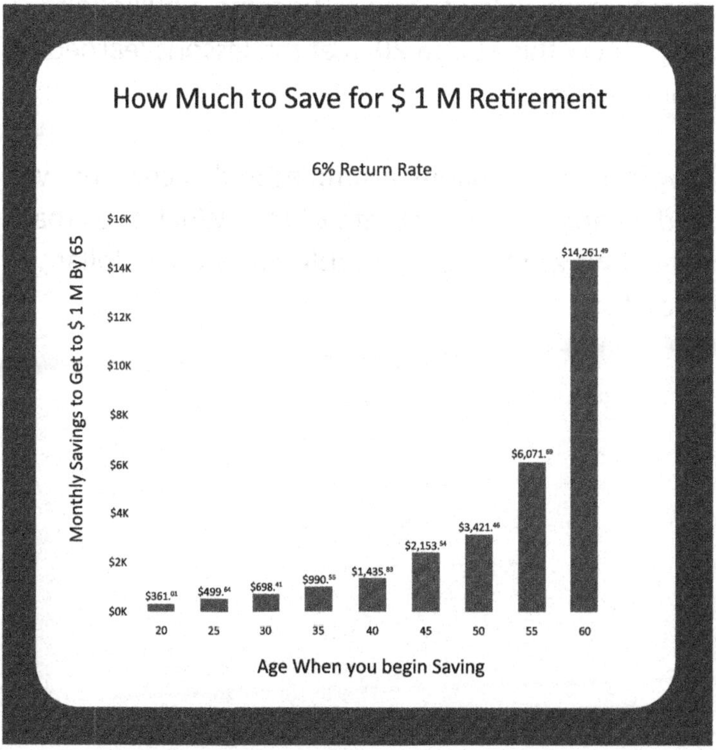

Notes:

1) The chart represents MONTHLY savings to get $1 million by the age of 65
2) Based on a 6% return rate

If we start at 20 years of age, then we only need to save $361.04 to become a millionaire at age 65. However, if we were to wait just 10 years before we started saving, the amount we would have to save every month almost doubles to $698.41. The amounts start to increase exponentially for every 10 years that we delay saving to become a millionaire. I wish I knew this at age 20. Let my lessons learned be your kickstart.

Now in all our previous examples in this chapter, we used a constant interest rate of 6%. What does that mean if we are trying to double our money dollar for dollar?

Table #3: Number of Years to Double Investment Value

Number of Years to Double Investment Value

Rate of Return	Years to Double	Rate of Return	Years to Double
25%	2.88	10%	7.20
20%	3.60	9%	8.00
19%	3.80	8%	9.00
18%	4.00	7%	10.20
17%	4.20	6%	12.00
16%	4.50	5%	14.40
15%	4.80	4%	18.00
14%	5.10	3%	24.00
13%	5.50	2%	36.00
12%	6.00	1%	72.00
11%	6.50		

(Robbins, MONEY, pp. 286)

Well, Table #3 tells us that for a 6% interest rate, it will take 12 years for us to double our income. In other words, if we had initially invested our $10,000 in the year 2000, by the year 2012, our nest egg at 6% interest would be worth $20,000 contingent on the fact that we did not add any additional funds to the account over that period. The higher the interest rate received, the less time it takes to double our investment. So, if we found ourselves constantly receiving 12% interest every year, it would take us only 6 years to double our investment. If we received a measly 2% interest each year (as is typically the case on a traditional CD account), it would take us 36 years to double our investment.

Once we become familiar with and actively start taking advantage of compound interest, there are several tools online to help us figure out variable compound interest over time, such as a compound interest calculator. The only information that we will need is to have what the current principal is on the account, our intended monthly addition, the number of years we need for the account to grow, the interest rate that the account will receive, and the number of times per year the compound interest would be applied to the account (yearly, quarterly, semiannually, etc.) The calculator would then be able to estimate the future value of the account to assure that the amount that we invest each month is on target to meet our financial goals.

Chapter 8:
Long-Term Investment Venues

We have covered the process of transferring our money habits from being pure consumers to becoming well-informed investors. We are equipped to become a sound financial steward and capable of becoming debt-free with the Budgeting in THREE Dimensions spreadsheet! We can control the hemorrhaging we used to have when it came to spending and having overwhelming debt. It is time to talk about options available to take our newly acquired savings account and transfer it into investment opportunities.

If we look at investing from the ground up, we should start by properly defining the possible investment venues that are available to put our monies toward. In the following chapters, we will also talk about a sound strategy that will maximize our returns. With the right proportion of these investment venues, we can structure a properly balanced and diversified portfolio. Why does the portfolio have to be properly balanced and diversified? Remember Warren Buffet's Rule #1: "Don't lose money!" If our portfolios are not balanced properly, this could have a devastating effect on our investments, especially if they occur early on in our investing adventure. Take, for example, the portfolios of Robert and Nicole.

In Chart #13 below, Robert and Nicole received the exact same returns on a starting portfolio of $500,000 from the time they were 65 years thru their retirement years. They withdrew the exact same amount each year for living expenses accounting for inflation each year. The only difference is that Robert's returns were in reverse order of Nicole's. Unfortunately, the first three years of investments were in the negative for Robert, whereas it happened the last three years for Nicole. As a result, Robert's losses upfront caused him to run out of his retirement savings at the age of 83, even though his portfolio only had negative returns 2 years afterward. By the time he was 83 years old, he was out of retirement money and had to go back to work at Walmart to finish out his retirement years. On the other hand, Nicole's retirement account grew substantially such that even though she had the same losses Robert had the last three years on her investment account, she still had a nest egg at the start of age 89 of $1.6 million!

Chart #11: Flip Flop Gains

Flip Flop Gains

Robert

Age	Gains or Losses	Withdrawl at Start of Year	Nest Egg at Start of Year
64			$500,000
65	-10.14%	$25,000	$500,000
66	-13.04%	$25,750	$426,839
67	-23.37%	$26,523	$348,766
68	14.62%	$27,318	$246,956
69	2.03%	$28,318	$251,750
70	12.40%	$28,982	$228,146
71	27.25%	$29,851	$223,862
72	-6.56%	$30,747	$246,879
73	26.31%	$31,669	$201,956
74	4.46%	$32,619	$215,084
75	7.06%	$33,598	$190,084
76	-1.54%	$34,606	$168,090
77	34.11%	$35,644	$131,429
78	20.26%	$36,713	$128,458
79	31.01%	$36,815	$110,335
80	26.67%	$38,949	$95,008
81	19.53%	$40,118	$71,009
82	26.38%	$36,923	$36,923
83	-38.49%	$0	$0
84	3.00%		
85	13.62%		
86	3.53%		
87	26.38%		
88	23.45%		
89	12.78%		

Nicole

Age	Gains or Losses	Withdrawl at Start of Year	Nest Egg at Start of Year
64			$500,000
65	12.78%	$25,000	$500,000
66	23.45%	$25,750	$535,716
67	26.38%	$26,523	$629,575
68	3.53%	$27,318	$762,140
69	13.62%	$28,318	$760,755
70	3.00%	$28,982	$832,396
71	-38.49%	$29,851	$827,524
72	26.38%	$30,747	$490,684
73	19.53%	$31,669	$581,270
74	26.67%	$32,619	$656,916
75	31.01%	$33,598	$790,788
76	20.26%	$34,606	$991,981
77	34.11%	$35,644	$1,151,375
78	-1.54%	$36,713	$1,496,314
79	7.06%	$37,815	$1,437,133
80	4.46%	$38,949	$1,498,042
81	26.31%	$40,118	$1,524,231
82	-6.56%	$41,321	$1,874,535
83	27.25%	$42,561	$1,712,970
84	12.40%	$48,383	$2,125,604
85	2.03%	$45,153	$2,339,923
86	14.62%	$46,507	$2,341,267
87	-23.37%	$47,903	$2,630,297
88	-13.04%	$49,340	$1,989,993
89	-10.14%	$50,820	$1,677,975

(Robbins, MONEY, pp. 419-422)

When speaking of investments, everyone has heard or knows about stocks and bonds. But do we know what the difference is between the two? Let's clear that up just in case. A stock is a type of security that signifies a certificate of ownership in a company or a corporation. It also represents a claim for us on a piece of any future assets and earnings that the corporation may accumulate. In other words, when you purchase stock, you are buying into the management, service, and product of the company. Now there are two primary types of stocks. The first type is called common stock, which entitles the owner to vote at all shareholder's meetings. This includes voting for new board members, company budget acceptance, and any other proxy that will have an impact on future operations or management of the company. The second type is called preferred stock. Preferred stock ownership does not have any voting rights associated with it, but it normally carries a higher claim on assets and earnings of the company. The owner serves more like a silent partner whose investments are rewarded when the company stock increases and/or dividends are awarded on a quarterly or semi-annual basis.

The key difference between a stock and a bond is where a stock presents ownership of a company, and a bond reflects a loan of the investor to a company or government agency.

There are four major categories when it comes to stock companies. The first category of stocks is blue-chip stocks. These are the stocks of large, well-established, and financially sound companies that have been operating successfully for many years. Examples of this are companies such as Walmart, Exxon, General Electric, and McDonald's. The second category of stocks is large-cap stocks. These stocks consist of companies that keep annual capital of over

$10 billion. Next are mid-cap stocks, which consist of companies with a market capitalization between $2-10 billion. Finally, there are small-cap stocks that have companies with capitalization between $300 million and $2 billion. All these stocks are traded and purchased on the stock markets such as the New York Stock Exchange (NYSE) or the National Association of Securities Dealers Automated Quotation System (NASDAQ), which is the global electronic marketplace for buying and selling securities as well as the benchmark index for the US technology stocks.

There are five kinds of stock according to how they generate and distribute profits to their shareholders:

1) Income Stocks: These are stocks of primarily stable companies that generally do not reinvest a big part of their profits back into the company each year. Most of their profits are distributed to their shareholders. If you are looking to make some income via dividends and capital appreciation, this kind of stock is the best to invest in. Current examples of income stocks are Microsoft Corporation (MSFT) which offers 2.7% dividends, and Cisco Systems Inc. (CSCO), which offers 2.9% dividends.

2) Growth Stocks: These are stocks of companies whose primary objective is to

obtain growth. With these companies, dividend income is usually small to nonexistent because the company is focusing all their earnings back into the company. Usually, the reason is that the company is just starting out, which makes it a much higher risk than income stocks. However, the long-term average annual growth is usually more than 10 percent. This is for the investors who are looking for a quick turnover in their profits but can afford the high risk that is associated with them. Examples of some current great growth stocks are Walt Disney (DIS) which offers investors the benefits of a blue-chip growth company with annualized 16% from 2016 to 2019; and Spirit Airlines Inc. (SAVE), which, as of March 2016, is generating a 5-year annual growth rate of 43% earnings per share.

3) Value Stocks: These stocks are ones that have been previously battered by the market fluctuation, but in management evaluation, they remain a good buy. A company's value is measured in terms of its solid management and the company's underlying assets such as cash, real estate, plants, and equipment. A value stock investor will buy stock based on the fact that they are getting shares of a solid

company at a good price, assuming that in time, the market will rebound and reflect that stock in its value price. Examples of current value stocks in emerging markets are Vivo of Brazil (VIV) which in 2018 is issuing dividend yields of over 8% with a trailing price to earnings ratio of 11.02 and the company's first-quarter net earnings margin around the same; and Embraer (ERJ) of Brazil, the fourth largest manufacturer of commercial aircraft which has a huge 7-year backlog and rapid increase in profits is expected to grow by more than 7% per year for the next decade.

4) Speculative Stocks: These are the riskiest stocks on the market. They are issued by relatively brand-new companies that very few established investors have heard of. Unless you are experienced in picking these stocks, I will suggest you avoid dealing with them altogether.

5) Cyclical Stocks: These stocks are for companies that are closely associated with the business cycle and the economy. These stocks are usually indicators of whether the market is in a growth phase or whether the economy is slowing down. If the economy is doing well and production is keeping pace with the increase of consumer

demand, then the earnings and prices for these stocks will probably rise. However, if the economy isn't doing well and consumers are turning back on new cars, then most likely, the earning and prices will fall. Examples of cyclical stocks are Amazon.com Inc. (AMZN) which is a revolutionary company that has changed its industry with top-line growth, which has appreciated 119% over the year in 2016 with an additional appreciation of 38% in 2017; and Netflix Inc. (NFLX) which is a disrupter with revenue growth consistently impressive with 69 million global subscribers with stock appreciation of 129%. Keep in mind that the companies listed above are prime snapshot examples and may not be the exact examples at the point of reading, but they illustrate key elements to look for with each kind of stock.

Open an emergency account in the form of a money market account. Saving anywhere between 3-6 months of your normal budget is served well by a money market account.

The key difference between a stock and a bond is whereas a stock presents ownership of a company, a bond reflects a loan of the investor to a company or government agency. A bond is a debt investment where the investor loans money to an entity that borrows the funds for a defined period at a variable or a fixed interest rate. Like stocks, there are two types of bonds available. The first is Government Bonds, where the government issues a treasury bond to hold your monies for a defined period for a guaranteed return on the monies rendered. The second is Corporate Bonds that are used to raise money to finance new projects within the company expansion versus obtaining loans from banks. All bonds have associated with it an interest rate and a maturity date. The keynote about bonds is that when interest rates decrease, the bond price increases. As an example, if you have a treasury bond issued at 5% at $1000 par value with a 5% annual coupon, the bond will generate a $50 cash flow per year to the bondholder. If the interest rate were to drop down to 4%, the bond would continue to pay the 5% increased option. This makes bonds very attractive for investors to purchase, and a bidding price war commences to a premium until the effective rate on the bond equals 4%. However, if the interest rate rises to 6%, the 5% coupon is no longer attractive to potential buyers. This causes the bond price to fall, which the bond will only sell at a discount until the effective rate of the bond is equivalent to 6%. Remember, when interest rates decrease, the bond price increases, and when interest rates increase, the bond price will decrease.

Now for a lot of people, this is where the investment world ends. However, there are a lot of other investment venues we should be made aware of, as adding them to our portfolio will help us achieve a risk-balanced portfolio protecting our investments in any market. The problem with just investing in stocks and bonds is that stocks are extremely volatile, and just as fast as stocks can go up, they will just as quickly come back down. Also, the year 2008 demonstrated a season where both stocks and bonds dropped at the same time, which was devastating to several investors who just invested in stocks and bonds. Let's go over the other investment venues that are available to us for investment purposes.

Let's look at the safest venues for investing and saving money. The first venue that everyone should have is a Money Market Account. A Money Market Account is an interest-bearing account that typically pays a higher interest rate than a savings account with a limited check-writing ability. Money Market Accounts behave more like a hybrid savings/checking account. I suggest having an emergency account in the form of a money market account. Saving anywhere between 3-6 months of your normal budget is served well by a money market account. They are offered by banks and other financial institutions. They require a higher minimum balance, and they are more liquid than bonds. Most banks usually invest the funds in Certificate of Deposits (CDs), Government Securities, and Commercial Paper. Now CDs are simply savings certificates entitling the bearer to receive interest, bear a maturity date and a specified fixed interest rate, and they are issued by commercial banks.

Market-linked CDs (MLCD) are specific types of CDs that are linked to the performance of one or more securities or market indexes. Indexed-linked CDs offer a potentially higher return than many other variations. They are high risk even though the initial investment will never be lost. As a comparison, traditional CDs may pay 0.23% or 23 basis points, whereas indexed-linked CDs allow you to participate in the upside paying 0.28% in addition to allowing you to participate in up to 5% of the market gains. All CDs possess no risk as well as are insured by the Federal Deposit Insurance Corporation (FDIC). The FDIC is a U.S. corporation that insures deposits in the United States against bank failure. It was created in 1933 to maintain public trust and encourage stability in the financial system with sound banking practices up to $250,000 per institution.

The next instrument on the list as a possible investment venue is annuities. An annuity is a contractual financial product that is sold by the bank, investment companies, or insurance companies designed to accept and grow funds from an individual over a defined period. Upon annuitization, the companies will pay out a stream of payments to the individual at a later point in time. There are two phases to an annuity: the accumulation phase and the annuitization phase. Now, most people want to forego the annuity due to false accusations about the annuity and its characteristics. The gambled rumor is that the individual invests all the monies into the annuity during the accumulation phase only to lose it by death way too soon. However, this is not the case if you use the right type of annuity and have it structured correctly.

There are two types of annuities: fixed and variable. Variable annuities allow the owner to receive much greater future cash flow if the investments of the annuity do well and will receive smaller payments if the investments do poorly as there is less stable cash available. My recommendation is DO NOT USE THIS ONE! But I must inform you that there are two types of annuities so that you will not be fooled into getting one. The one I would recommend is the fixed annuity. The fixed annuity provides regular, periodic payments to the individual once the annuitization phase begins. Even better is the Fixed Index Annuity (FIA). FIAs are bench-marked to a stock market index such as the NASDAQ or the S&P500. FIAs offer the ability to create an income stream that the individual cannot possibly outlive. This translates into a paycheck for life serving as a personal pension.

The IRA is an investing tool used by individuals to earn and earmark funds specifically for retirement. The key distinction it has is the ability to tax-defer income, which becomes a very valuable tax management tool that can be used for extensive tax savings.

FIAs will not exceed or fall below the specified return levels even if the underlying stock indices fluctuate outside of the index annuity's growth rate and caps. In other words, the insurance company that is sponsoring the annuity bears the risk of a sharp stock market decline with this type of annuity. As an investor, you cannot lose any of your principal with a fixed index annuity, and your potential gains are usually capped at a rate between 3% and 9%. Many fixed index annuities also offer premium bonuses, but usually at the expense of lower potential gains. FIAs offer a high degree of safety to your portfolio. Insurance companies are legally required to set aside assets or reserves to cover potential claims made by their policyholders. There are several advantages to having an FIA. We will explore these more when we talk in more detail about long-term investment venues.

The next venue we need to define is the Individual Retirement Account (IRA). The IRA is an investing tool used by individuals to earn and earmark funds specifically for retirement. The key distinction it has is the ability to tax-defer income, which becomes a very valuable tax management tool that can be used for extensive tax savings. There are three different types of personal IRAs that we need to be concerned about here.

1) The Traditional IRA: This IRA is a tax-deferred account that allows us to invest a finite amount into the account each year without any taxes applied until we

withdraw it at retirement. Then a one-time tax is applied at the time of withdrawal. This allows us to grow our investments at much faster pace over time until its necessity at retirement.

2) The Roth IRA: This IRA was created in the year 1996 for investors to make the most of their returns. As opposed to the Traditional IRA, the Roth IRA calls for us to pay taxes on the investment one time in the year of the investment. Afterward, no more taxes are paid ever on the account to include all the gains made on the account. All gains are tax-free.

How does that differ from investing in the Traditional IRA? The critical difference, in my opinion, is the amount of time we have until retirement. If retirement for you is 10 years or less, then the Traditional IRA may be the best venue. The accumulation of cash is critical as retirement is just around the corner. By deferring taxes on your investment will allow you to achieve your cashflow. However, if your retirement date is more than 10 years away, the scales start to flip such that the Roth IRA is the better venue. Paying your taxes upfront will allow your gains to accumulate over time. The more time that you have before you can withdraw the funds, the more time your gains can build in your account.

There is a third IRA account that is not well known but can be a tremendous boost to your retirement portfolio.

3) The Self-Directed IRA: This IRA is a special fund that only a handful of companies are certified to execute. It is a retirement account that sets up a trust fund where our investments carry the ability to fund a business, a second home, or real estate. The key to it is that any returns or profits that come as a result of the investment are owned and must be deposited back into the trust. So, if we purchase a second house and rent out the house to a tenant, all rental payments from that tenant have to be deposited into the trust account. We will not be able to access any of the gains ourselves until we reach the retirement requirements. Any business that we invest in must be a corporation or a limited liability company. The company that I use is named Equity Trust (www.trustetc.com) out of Westlake, Ohio. They will assist you with any transaction that you may have to ensure that it meets all the requirements of a Self-Directed IRA. For example, if we buy a house using 50% from the Self-Directed account and 50% from our own individual funds from another source, then the

contract would be set up so that the Trust would own 50% of the house, and we would own 50% of the house. From that day forward, any money paid from renting the house, 50% of the payment will go to the Trust, and 50% will come to us.

In addition to having a retirement account that we can set up ourselves, there are also retirement plans if you are employed by varying-sized businesses. If you work for a small business, there is the SIMPLE IRA (Savings Incentive Match Plan for Employees of Small Employers). This venue allows the employer to receive tax deductions by contributing to the employee's SIMPLE plan up to 3% or a 2% non-elective contribution regardless of whether the employee contributes or not. There is also the Simplified Employee Pension (SEP) IRA, where the employee will contribute to receive a pension at the point of retirement. Pension funds used to be managed by employers, and they paid out a steady income over the course of the retirement. (If you have a government job or a strong union, you may still be eligible for a pension.)

The newer retirement plans that were set up to replace pension plans and put the burden of retirement on the individual are 401K plans. They were established in the year 1978, allowing employees to create and control their own pension. 401(k) plans, named for the section of the tax code that governs them, arose during the 1980s as a supplement to pensions. The 401K plan is established for the qualified employer, usually a large corporation, to extend to eligible employees to make salary deferral contributions on a pre/post-tax basis. Employers may make matching or non-elective contributions to the plans that include profit-sharing features. Taxes aren't paid until the money is withdrawn from the account. The 401K was upgraded to include a traditional and a Roth 401k in the year 2006. The traditional 401K and the Roth 401K apply the same rules as does the IRAs. For Traditional IRAs and 401Ks, the employee's wages are contributed before taxes from each paycheck, like a deferred salary. The employee's taxable income drops by the amount contributed.

The employee pays income taxes on contributions and earnings upon withdrawal at retirement, which is declared at age 59 1/2 or age 55 if you leave your employer. Otherwise, expect a 10% penalty on top of your usual tax bill if you withdraw early. For Roth IRAs and Roth 401Ks, all contributions are made with money that's already been taxed.
There are no taxes paid upon withdrawal for any of the investments or the gains in the account. As far as the withdrawal rules, there is much better flexibility with the Roth versus the Traditional. If you have held the Roth account for 5 years or more, you have free access to your money.

TIPS are government treasuries that are indexed specifically to inflation in order to protect investors from the negative effects of inflation. Since they are backed by the US government, they carry extremely low risk.

For retirement accounts, people who work for non-profit organizations have the 403b plan, also known as a tax-sheltered annuity (TSA) plan. For people who work for higher educational institutions, there is the 457 Plan which serves as the retirement vehicle for state government employees and employees of state educational institutions as well as private educational institutions. Finally, the people who are looking to invest in someone's higher education, there is the 529 plan, which is a tax-advantaged investment vehicle in the United States for each state that encourages saving for the future education of a designated beneficiary. The only drawback is that money must be applied to a school that is in the state of your current residence.

The next long-term investment venue I need to highlight is the Treasury Inflation Protected Securities (TIPS). TIPS are government treasuries indexed specifically to inflation to protect investors from the negative effects of inflation. Since they are backed by the US government, they carry extremely low risk. They also have a fixed interest rate, and the par value of the adjusted principal and interest payments rise with inflation as measured by the Consumer Price Index (CPI). Why do we need to pay attention and plan for inflation with our financial portfolio? Chart #14 shows how inflation has affected various categories that we depend on in our everyday lives. Take special note of how much college tuition and fees have risen since 1975.

Chart #14: Inflation Comparison: Percent Growth

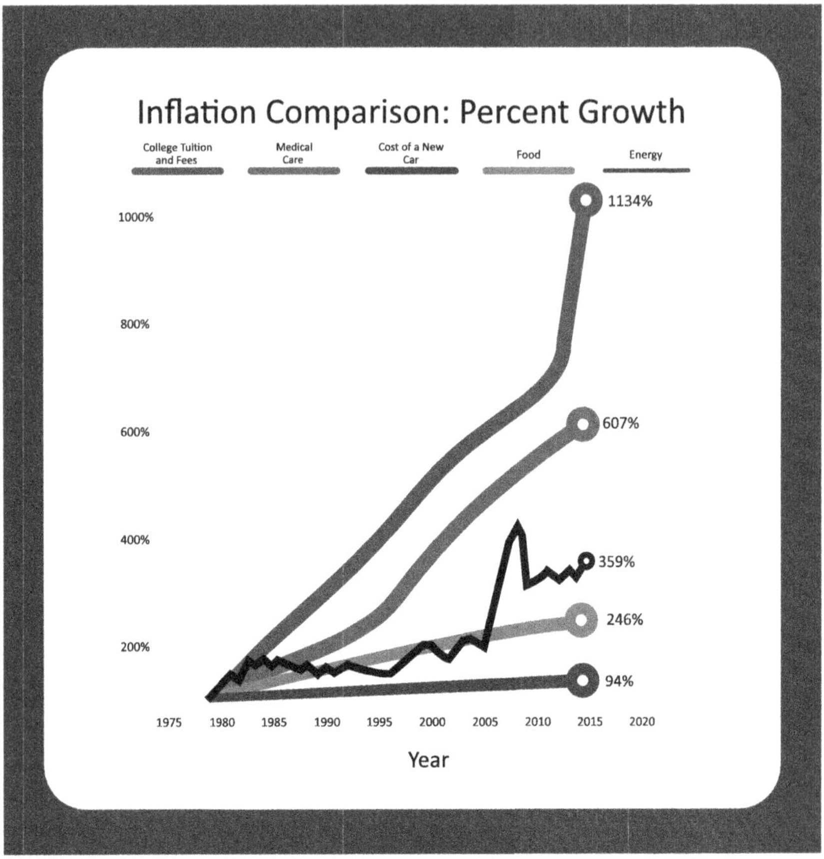

TIPS pays interest semiannually and can be purchased from Treasury Direct in $100 increments with 5, 10, or 30-year maturity rates. You can also hold TIPS in a related mutual fund or tax-deferred retirement account to avoid tax implications as well as avoid management fees associated with standard mutual funds. TIPS is also exempt from state and local taxes.

ETFs are security tracking sets of equities, commodities, and bonds, like an index traded as normal shares of stock in a similar industry on the stock exchange.

There are Real Estate Investment Trusts (REITs) that allow for investors to delve into real estate investments that may be better served with a group of investors. REITs are securities that invest in real estate through property or mortgages and often trade on major exchanges, typically offering high dividend yields. REITs can include anything from commercial properties, apartment complexes, hospitals, office buildings, timberland, and shopping malls. For a typical REIT, 75% of its holdings and assets must be in real estate; the law requires at least a 90% dividend payout, which makes REITs a favorite for income-seeking investors.

The final venue that I will describe for you is the Exchange Traded Fund (ETF) Stock. ETFs are a new way of purchasing stocks in basket form. ETFs are security tracking sets of equities, commodities, and bonds, like an index traded as normal shares of stock in a similar industry on the stock exchange. ETFs trade like common stock on the stock exchange, and they experience price changes throughout the day as they are bought and sold. ETFs come in the form of stocks, taxable bonds, specific sectors, municipal bonds, international stocks, commodities, and balanced for intermediate-term investors. There is also another form of ETF called Leveraged ETFs, which are highly speculative short-term investments and are different from the other ETFs mentioned. These ETFs use leverage as they borrow to increase the amount that they can invest in the market. This makes them much riskier than funds that do not borrow, but I must make you aware of these as they aim to double or triple the daily return of a specified index. In summary, ETFs are a combination of many different investment assets.

Chapter 9:

To Beat or Mimic the Market?

All investors have the desire to find a way to beat the market and maximize their returns in the shortest period possible. But having the discipline and the foresight to beat the market is a different story. Brokers are always advertising that they have the perfect formula that will beat the market every time. But is beating the market realistic? Is there even a possibility of being able to beat the market year after year after year without any period of loss in between? In my opinion, being that the stock market can be so erratic and unpredictable at times, along with the fact that beating the market often depends on the results of the market itself, raises doubt as to how realistic beating the market is. History has shown that during the period of 1984 thru 1998, only 8 out of 200 mutual funds were able to beat the market for any sustainable period. Maybe, it is because their strategy is all wrong. If we are so dependent on the market reacting favorably to maximize any gain, why not set up our portfolio to mimic the market instead of beating it?

My recommendation is to follow the vessels that mimic the market- Index Funds. Index Funds basically mirror the images of the index that they represent.

Investing is a lot like boxing- Counterintuitive! When a boxer punches their opponent, they step away from the punch to keep from stepping into the opponent's punch. Our normal instincts would say that we should step into the punch. But stepping into the punch makes you more vulnerable to a counter punch, especially if your punch doesn't land properly. Well, the same principle goes for investing. As an investor, to be successful, you must be able to act against the grain of the public norm. When public emotion is high, and they are flooding to the buying market, it is probably best to sell; when public emotion is panicked and wants to "ill-advisedly" pull out of the market, it is best to buy into the market. The public emotion causes people who react along with it to buy high and sell low (not a good way to make money in the market). The successful investor operates counterintuitively by buying low and selling high (a great way to make money in the market).

My recommendation is to follow the vessels that mimic the market- Index Funds. Index Funds basically mirror the images of the index that they represent. There are index funds that mirror the Standard and Poor's (S&P) 500 Index. Or there are index funds that mirror the Dow Jones Index or the Technology Index. We could also follow an Emerging Markets Stock Index or Developed (Foreign) Markets Index. But many mutual fund managers try to find ways to beat these index markets. Yet, they find that the daunting task is more difficult than they might have considered. From 1993 thru 2013 (20 years), the S&P 500 return an annual average of 9.28%. However, the average mutual fund investor only made just over 2.54% which is an 80% difference! I had my lessons learned when I first started investing with mutual funds. In the 1990s, I called myself being very smart. I found a mutual fund company that advertised that they were always looking to beat the market with the different funds they provided. In the last couple of years, they had a decent return on most of their funds, so they looked very attractive. One of the main points that put me over the top with them was that all of their portfolio fund managers were Ivy League graduates (Dartmouth, Princeton, and Columbia were the ones managing the funds I chose). I did dollar cost averaging with them from 1993 thru 2008. Within that period, the yearly statements depicted that my portfolio had made 6.53%, but somehow, even with the no-load fees, the net result of my portfolio after 2008 was a mere 2.75%!

One of the main issues that people have that works against them when it comes to investing is that they like funds or strategies of funds that make them look flashy. The concept of beating the market feeds to that flashy feel. That is why people love to invest in technology or aggressive stocks that give signs that a quick and fluid return is inevitable if we can only time it correctly. Well, timing the market is never a good strategy because it is never clear when the market will take off or if it becomes clear, it is often too late. I mention this to say that a great investor is, for the most part, is a boring investor. They don't look to beat the market, but only participate in what the market has to offer. They are not trying to time the market but become a regular investor that diversifies their portfolio and often does dollar-cost averaging. Dollar-cost averaging is the process of investing at regular intervals during the year regardless of what the market is doing, keeping the percentages of their diversified portfolio in constant proportions.

As an example, an investor desires to keep the portfolio balanced at 30% stocks, 30% bonds, 20% Treasury Inflation Protected Securities (TIPS), and 20% commodities. The investor contributes $1000 each month proportioned in each category regardless of what the market is doing or what current state it is in (bull or bear market). If, after six months, he realizes gains that take his portfolio out of balance to where it is now 45% stocks, 30% bonds, 15% TIPS, and 10% commodities, he will proceed to sell his stocks and shift those gains to buy more TIPS and commodities until his portfolio is once again balanced in accordance with his portfolio percentage plan.

I was not aware of the power of the index fund until figuring out my lessons learned of my "beat the market mutual fund" years. As I stated earlier, index funds are mirrors of the market that they represent. Because they mimic their market instead of attempting to beat it means a couple of things for the investor. First, they do not trade nearly as much as managers who are trying to beat the market. This means that there are a lot of less transaction fees to pay, and you best believe that these transaction fees are being paid from our accounts. This is probably the biggest reason my mutual fund only gave me a 2.75% return versus the 6.53% advertised in the previous example. Second, the market represents us and our economic reach which allows us to base the market on the state of the consumers in our country. If we are reluctant to go out and spend for the necessities in home life, then the economic trending market will in some way reflect that. However, if we are making aggressive plans to do home improvements to our home because we have the extra spending capital, somewhere, the market will reflect that. It is not a way to accurately predict the market's next move, but it will give us an idea of how to invest in it. Invest in what you know!

We must build a system of investing that is independent of emotional strain that minimizes risk and satisfies our long-term goals, which is a portfolio that has long-term sustained growth.

The main reason that we cannot accurately predict what the market is going to do next is that the market reaction is not solely based on economic performances. It is also heavily influenced by emotional oscillations of people investing. Chart #15 illustrates the full sinusoidal curving function of how emotions oscillate from the point of maximum financial risk to the point of maximum financial opportunity.

Chart #15: Sine Curve of Emotions

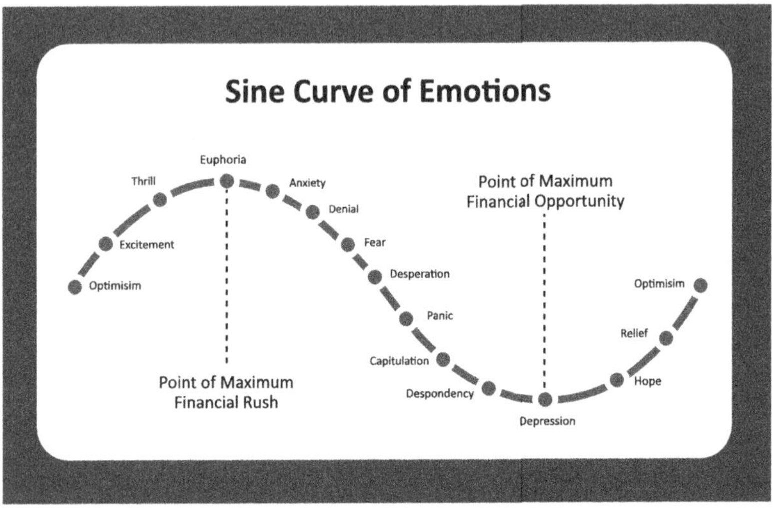

(Robbins, MONEY, pp. 96)

The best way to accomplish a system of long-term sustained growth is to place our investments so that the foundation of our portfolio mimics the market.

Earlier, I stated that to be an effective investor, we must invest in the opposite fashion of what the norm is doing. Every new investor starts at the stage of Optimism. Just the opportunity to make money on their initial investment immediately brings them the excitement. If a stock shows substantial growth over a small period, it becomes newsworthy and advertised on CNBC, meaning it has already experienced most of its growth. Yet, the history of the stock brings our emotional investors to the point of Euphoria. This stage correlates with the point of maximum financial risk. If a person is investing mostly on the point of their emotions, they are putting themselves in a position most vulnerable to losing their investments in part or in totality. Then the moment happens.

The stock price starts to decline. As the price drops exponentially, the emotions of the investor fall through the stages of Anxiety, Denial, and Fear. Could this really be happening to them? There was so much Optimism when they started this new fad called investing.
Now, their money is slipping out of their fingers as they speak. There is a point to be made here. As the emotions pass through this stage, no money has been lost yet because the stock has not been sold yet. It is still the piece of paper that represents an investment that has not been valued yet. But emotions can cause you to process it as if the paper already has been valued. Then the stages of Desperation and Panic set in, and the risk tolerance of the person has maximized, and they proceed to sell the stock. The only problem is that the stock was bought at a high value and now is being sold at a low value. Now enter the emotional periods of Capitulation, Despondency, and Depression. Reality kicks in that the stock was sold way too soon. Yet, we are at the point of

maximum financial opportunity. This is the point where everyone is selling, but you, being the savvy investor, should be buying. Suddenly, the stock rebounds and starts climbing out of the hole back to new heights. This brings the emotions of Hope and Relief, which brings most investors the light bulb that maybe I should get back into the investment game as it looks like the market will recover. Now we are back at the emotional stage of Optimism once again.

Chart #16: Gain Required to Break Even

Gain Required to Break Even

If You Lose	Gain Required to Break Even
5%	5%
10%	11%
15%	18%
20%	25%
25%	33%
30%	43%
35%	54%
40%	67%
45%	82%
50%	100%
75%	300%
90%	900%

(Robbins, MONEY, pp. 405)

The key is we must build a system of investing that is independent of emotional strain that minimizes risk, and satisfies our long-term goals, which is a portfolio that has long-term sustained growth.

Remember Warren Buffet's Rule #1: "Don't lose money!" Why does this statement keep coming up in conversation? What happens if we do lose money? Look at it from the standpoint of how much it takes to get it back. If we look at Chart #16, we realize how much it takes in the required gain just to break even.

If we lose 5% of our investment, it will take a gain of 5% to break even. However, the more we lose, the gain required to break even starts to go up exponentially to where if we lose 90% of our investment, it will take 900% gains to break even again. The best way to accomplish a system of long-term sustained growth is to place our investments so that the foundation of our portfolio mimics the market. In order to build a system of investing so that the foundation mimics the market, we must do two things. First, we must review and follow The Seven Methodical Steps to Creating Capital for Investment from Chapter 4 that will allow us to invest effectively; next, we must take the eight steps to start down the road to investing and wealth.

Eight Steps to Start Your Road to Investing and Wealth

1. Setup a Brokerage Account
2. Transfer Initial Funds (Savings Account) over to a Money Market Account to serve as your emergency fund (6 months' worth of financial security expenses)
3. Start an automated transfer of a minimum of $50 per month (preferably $100 if possible) into the Money Market Account.
4. Accumulate funds into the Money Market until $3000 has been achieved
5. Invest funds into an Index Market Fund (1. S&P 500; 2. Treasury Bond Fund 3. Emerging Markets Fund)
6. Seek to find an Independent Fiduciary to help diversify funds once $10,000 has been accumulated in your investments
7. Continue to commit to investing and grow your nest egg based on your knowledge and comfort with the stocks and bonds market.
8. Start investing in Long-Term Investment Venues to minimize tax obligations and set up for retirement goals

Let's talk about the eight steps here:

1) Setup a Brokerage Account: Once we start to develop and mature a discipline to put aside monies for investment purposes and

to grow our investment egg, we will need a brokerage account to put the monies in so that we can better dictate where the monies need to be invested. We can then easily transfer those monies into the investment accounts. I personally use Vanguard Securities so that I have access to their index accounts. You may also want to investigate using TIAA-CREF or possibly Charles Schwab. I recommend these because their index funds have performed well over the past 20-30 years. They also have great access online, which makes it easy to track your fund performance.

2) Transfer Initial Funds over to a Money Market Account for Emergency Purposes: Money Market Funds are great venues to place monies that can be liquidated very easily and very quickly, but at the same time gain us a decent rate of return while our money is in the account. The brokerage accounts will have a money market fund available for us. Some brokerage accounts require us to have anywhere from $1000 to $4000 in our account before we can invest in an index fund. The money market account helps us build up our capital until we have that capability.

3) Start an Automated Transfer of a Minimum of $50 per month: Automated transfers allow us to keep up the discipline of investing on regular intervals with consistency. My suggestion of $50 per month should be a goal, but whatever amount that you can afford is acceptable. Even $10 per month helps us keep the discipline of investing every month but will not get us to our financial goals as fast. Whatever amount we can afford to put aside will help us get there over time.

4) Accumulate Funds into your Brokerage Account until $3000 is achieved: In most of my brokerage accounts, I need a minimum of $3000 in the account before I can invest in a specific fund. The goal is to accumulate this amount so that you can make better investments into your accounts.

5) Invest Funds into an Index Market Fund: At this point, we are ready to put our hard-earned money to work for us. Ask the brokerage firm that you are interested in for a prospectus and determined which index fund is the best one for you and your risk tolerances.

6) Seek an Independent Fiduciary to help Diversify your Portfolio and Financial Advice: Once you have accumulated at least $10,000 in your portfolio, it is now time to properly diversify your portfolio with a Strategic Percentage Plan of investments. The Fiduciary can help you ensure that your portfolio does not get out of balance due to revenues that you may have gained over the course of a year. Not rebalancing your portfolio will leave you vulnerable to situations where the market may fall or correct itself, and your gains suddenly vanish. We will talk about this in more detail in the upcoming chapters.

7) Commit to Investing and Growing your Nest Egg: Cycling the previous six steps on a regular basis requires a commitment to investing and creating wealth. All you need is time for your efforts to pay off and show themselves accordingly.

8) Start Investing in Long-Term Investment Venues to minimize tax obligations and set up for retirement goals: Our whole purpose in investing and making our nest egg increase is to set ourselves up for the retirement we really want and to have legacy capital to pass on to the next generation of family members. In order to

do that, we must reduce our taxes and invest the difference as well as set up for our retirement. This long-term planning will be addressed in the upcoming chapters.

Regarding Step#6 above, I should make mention that in the process of finding an independent fiduciary, it is important to understand the differences between an independent fiduciary and a broker, as illustrated in Chart #17.

Chart #17: Broker versus Independent Fiduciary

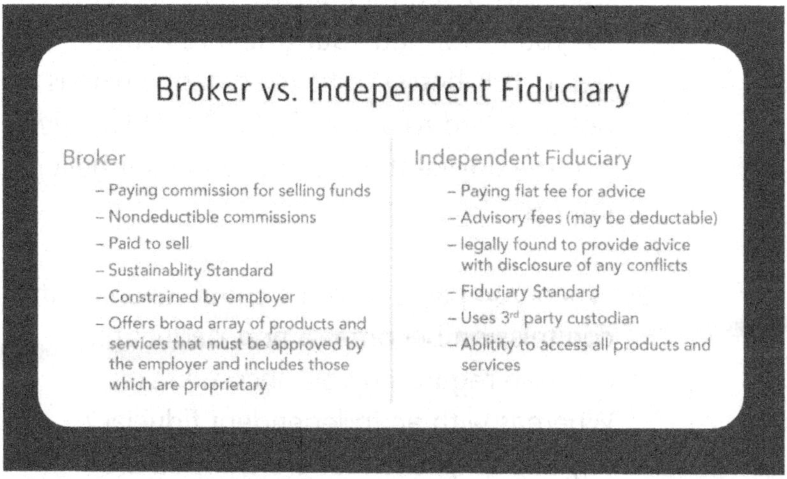

(Robbins, MONEY, pp. 139)

There are four fundamental differences that we need to be aware of when picking someone to help manage your money.

1) A broker often makes his commission by selling shares into a specific set of funds affiliated with the brokerage company that he works for, whereas an independent fiduciary will charge a flat fee for advice and a minimum percentage for managing your portfolio. What does that mean for you? A pressured broker will try to sell you on the hottest fund that is going around that is beating the market and is a shoo-in for the next year. Their company has an agreement with the fund to bring in new customers with a nice commission attached to it. However, their advice and decision for you never had your true interest at heart. It is better to have someone who is not attached to a specific fund that will give you the advice that you need in your best interest.

2) When you pay a broker's commission, that commission becomes a non-deductible expense regarding your income taxes. Whereas with an independent fiduciary, any advisory fees that are charged are deductible in most cases. Although you would have to check with your tax attorney or tax accountant to verify if they are indeed tax deductible, this benefit is only possible with the independent fiduciary, not the broker.

3) The broker gets paid by his brokerage firm to sell whatever fund is on the menu. This is often a conflict of interest with your interests as an investor. The independent fiduciary by contract is legally bound to provide you sound financial advice that is in your best interest and is required to disclose anything in your agreement that may present a conflict.

4) A broker often acts as the official custodian of your investment account, which once again may be a conflict of interest with your own investment goals. They will offer a broad array of products and services that may even have to be approved by your employer if you are in a 401k arrangement which includes those which are proprietary and may include your account without your say so. An independent fiduciary always uses a third party to serve as a custodian to your account, and they could access any products and services that may be vested into only with your approval. Finally, all independent fiduciaries should be members of the Registered Investment Advisor (RIA) and tracked by the Financial Industry Regulation Authority (FINRA). They are never referred to as "brokers" but

are registered representatives, financial advisors, or wealth advisors. With regards to their advisory fees, you should pay no more than 1.25% in annual advisory fee and less than 1% if you are only using their services as a portfolio manager. Every suggestion that they advise you on should have your best investments interests at heart.

Chart #18: Wall Street's Responses to the Fall of Enron

Wall Street on Enron

Date	Recommendation	Stock Value	Broker
21 Mar 2001	"Near Term Buy"	$55.89	Merrill Lynch
29 Mar 2001	"Recommend List"	$55.31	Goldman Sachs
08 Jun 2001	"Buy"	$47.26	J.P. Morgan
15 Aug 2001	"Strong Buy"	$40.25	Bank of America
04 Oct 2001	"Buy"	$33.10	A.G. Edwards
12 Nov 2001	"Strong Buy Attractive"	$16.41	Lehman Bros.
21 Nov 2001	"Hold"	$9.24	Prudential
29 Nov 2001	"Market Perform"	$5.01	Goldman Sachs
02 Dec 2001	"Hold"	$0.36	Credit Suisse First Boston
02 Dec 2001	"Oops - Bankrupt!"	$0.00	Enron-Chap II

(Robbins, MONEY, pp. 137)

Why don't all financial advisors or brokers have your best interests at heart? Well, in my opinion, Enron, a premier energy company, gives a good example of how being under pressure to sell whatever fund is on your book can cause brokers that do not have your best interest at heart to totally miscalculate the behavior of the market. If you look at Chart #16, the comments made about Enron when they cooked their books and were suddenly in severe financial trouble from March thru December 2001. In March, Enron's stock value was at $55.89 per share. Brokers were quoting it as a "Near Term Buy."

By June, it had dropped to $47.26 per share. Brokers were quoting it as a "Recommend List" and a "Buy." Mind you that these were quotes coming from brokerage companies such as Merrill Lynch, Goldman Sachs, and J.P. Morgan. By October, it had dropped continuously down to $33.10 per share; yet it received views such as "Strong Buy" by Bank of America. In November, it plunged down to $5.01 per share; yet it was still getting recommendations such as "Strong Buy, Attractive," "Hold," and "Market Perform."

Finally, its last listing in December was at $0.36 per share with a recommendation of "Hold" before the company finally declared Chapter 11 towards the end of that same day. How could all these major brokerage firms possibly miss the fact that Enron had no more cash flow within their business? Once again, it shows the tremendous pressures that brokers are under where it is easy for them to fail at forecasting these trends, which is not in your best interests. An independent fiduciary is the way to go.

Chapter 10:

The Seven Steps to Building Up Your Investment Portfolio

In the last chapter, we discussed in detail the advantages of having an independent fiduciary to assist you in your financial planning and the eight steps needed to break our cycle of being a lifetime consumer. We can now start creating habits that will convert our lifestyle to become informed investors. We are on the road to start accumulating wealth. What do we need to do to maintain that momentum? Can we confidently build up our investment portfolio? The last step of investing in long-term venues, these last two chapters will lay down the framework to accomplish our build-up and allow us to enter the wealth realm.

There are seven distinct steps that need to be adhered to for the next phase of our wealth build-up.

1) Build an emergency fund via a money market fund that will pay basic expenses for 3-6 months.
2) Open an Index Fund account and contribute 10% of earnings with the goal to increase to

20% or a percentage that meets your long-term goals.

3) If you have an employer, open a 401k/ Roth 401K and contribute up to the matching percentage of the employer contribution.
4) Open a Traditional/ Roth IRA and contribute the maximums allowed each year
5) If you are a small business owner, use Cash Balance (CB) plans to store cash in excess of the 401K plan.
6) Open an extremely low-cost fixed annuity with a list of low-cost index funds.
7) Open a Vanguard or Charles Schwab brokerage account to fulfill the remaining gold, commodities, and stock requirements.

Keep in mind that accomplishing these seven steps will not happen overnight. As a matter of fact, these seven steps will become our lifelong journey to retirement. The sooner that we can get started on accomplishing these steps, the better off and the more successful our retirement will be. So, let's briefly hit each step and the rationale behind each one.

1) Build an emergency fund via a money market fund that will pay basic expenses for 3-6 months: We touched on this one briefly in Chapter 8 while discussing money market funds. The premise of an emergency fund is to keep the funds accessible and easily liquidated just in case

of an emergency, such as a loss of a job, medical, or other financial burdens that may occur requiring immediate cash. That is why we have associated emergency funds with the money market fund. If an emergency does occur, we can have peace of mind knowing that we are covered for 3-6 months without missing a beat. Now I am also aware that building an emergency fund has been listed on the myth list regarding achieving wealth. I do agree that it is not a necessity in order to accumulate wealth. However, neither is purchasing auto or life insurance. It is very important for establishing peace of mind on your journey. We should view the emergency fund as an insurance policy towards our wealth in retirement.

2) Open an Index Fund account and contribute 10% of earnings with the goal to increase to 20% or a percentage that meets your long-term goals: I believe in giving 10% of our income in tithes and charity with the intention of helping other people. But I also believe in giving 10% to pay yourself! We work hard to obtain our earnings, and we should be awarded for it—what better way than to pay ourselves and then invest that money to work for us. I recommend an index fund based on the

concept of Chapter 9 in mimicking the market. Create the habit of setting aside 10% just for this. Then, as you get better at managing your finances using our Budgeting in THREE Dimensions spreadsheet, shoot for the goal of increasing that investment to 20% or a percentage that will help you meet your retirement goals.

3) Open a 401k/ Roth 401K and contribute up to the matching percentage of the employer contribution: This step is very critical and drawing free money to your retirement account. Most employers that offer 401Ks will match your investment up to 3% of your salary. There are some employers that will offer up to as much as 8-10% of your salary. This is additional money that you do not have to lay out a finger for, so take advantage. Traditional and Roth 401Ks allow up to $17,500 annual contributions.

4) Open a Traditional/ Roth IRA and contribute the maximums allowed each year: The IRA serves as the supplement to the 401K or as the prime retirement vehicle if your employer does not have a 401K plan. The IRS allows us to contribute up to $5,500 annually to IRAs. However,

single people who make $122,000 per year are not eligible to use a Roth IRA. However, there is no income limitation for Roth 401ks. Also, keep in mind the principles of whether to use a Traditional or Roth account, as we discussed in Chapter 8.

5) As a small business owner, use Cash Balance (CB) plans to store cash in excess of the 401K plan: In order to obtain larger tax deductions than 401Ks and IRAs can offer, a CB can be the supplementary source to accelerate our retirement savings as small business owners. They also serve as an alternative benefit plan for employees to receive a vested portion of their account balances. Chart #19 shows how much additional contributions can be added to the Cash Balance Plan and be accepted as a part of the IRS annual contribution for tax deductions. It also shows how much tax savings can result by using the Cash Balance Plan.

Chart #19: IRS Annual Contribution Limits (2016)

IRS Annual Contribution Limits (2016)

Age	401K Contribution & Profit Sharing Plan	Cash Balance Plan Contrbution	Total	Tax Savings
65	$59,000	$237,000	$296,000	$133,200
60	$59,000	$228,000	$287,000	$129,150
55	$59,000	$175,000	$234,000	$105,300
50	$59,000	$133,000	$192,000	$86,400
45	$53,000	$102,000	$155,000	$69,750
40	$53,000	$78,000	$131,000	$58,950
35	$53,000	$59,000	$112,000	$50,400

(Robbins, MONEY, pp. 159)

6) <u>Open an extremely low-cost fixed annuity with a list of low-cost index funds</u>: Fixed annuities have 100% principal protection guaranteed by the insurance company that offers it. This gives the fixed annuity an upside without a true downside. All gains taxes are deferred unless we set up the annuity within a Roth IRA. The key factor to an annuity is that it gives us the ability to create an income stream that we can't outlive with returns that mimic the market!

7) <u>Open a Vanguard or Charles Schwab brokerage account to fulfill remaining</u>

gold, commodities, and stock requirements: In the upcoming chapter, we will talk about how these remaining investment items will be critical in maintaining a low-risk balanced portfolio and the importance that they hold in countering all of the economic seasons that can occur. If our portfolio is balanced incorrectly, this could cause us to lose a significant amount of our investment during low tides. We can't have that! Once again, as Warren Buffett's #1 rule states, "Don't lose money!"

Chapter 11:

Investing in The Stock Market

As we approach the point of revealing what our portfolios should look like, it would suit us best to talk about how investing in stocks and bonds work in the marketplace. The stock market is simply an exchange where people buy and sell shares of company stock based on an opportunity to invest their money and make a profit from it. The list of possible stock options out there is tremendous. There are so many companies out there to choose from to the point it can look overwhelming. My advice is if you decide that you want to delve into the stock market on your own, then work with companies that you already know in your everyday life. If you frequently shop at Walmart, then Walmart should be on your list of options. If you are constantly taking the kids to McDonald's for a dinner treat, then McDonald's should be a part of your market. If you are a long-time customer of Bank of America, then they should be a part of your consideration. If you go with what you already know, then your stock market suddenly shrinks down to 10-15 stocks that you would consider investing in. Also, let me emphasize that investing in the stock market in this form should come after we have already established our investments, as we spoke of in Chapter 10. Investing in stocks in this fashion should constitute no more than 2-5% of our complete portfolio.

Investing in individual stocks is the riskiest of all investments. We either ride or die along with the company that we are investing in. If the company dies, we want to ensure that all our hard-earned investments do not die with it. A wise investor, who requires a lot of patience, can gather information to make wise decisions and must know what his tolerance base is. One rule of thumb regarding the stock market is that the stock prices go up or down not because of good or bad company management per se, but more primarily to supply and demand. Therefore, if there is abundant demand for the product, the prices will tend to go up; if there is an abundant supply, the prices will tend to go down. Stock prices tend to display a sinusoidal curve over time, so their gradual rise will fluctuate up and down as time continues.

Let's talk about the different stock markets. There are many different stock markets in the US and throughout the globe. The main stock market in the US is the New York Stock Exchange (NYSE) or sometimes referred to as Wall Street. There is also the American Stock Exchange (AMEX) which was added to the NYSE and merged with the Euronext, which consists of the NYSE Amex Equities and the NYSE Euronext. While the NYSE continues its traditional pattern of buying and selling stocks, the AMEX has evolved into a market for specialty products. In addition, there is the National Association of Securities Dealers Automated Quotations (NASDAQ) which is an electronic stock market tracking approximately 4000 technology-oriented market-weighted stocks. When a privately held corporation decides to go public, usually to raise money in order to grow bigger and better, they will issue an initial public offering (IPO) to offer common stock to the general public. The corporation will publish a stock offering to public markets by going through a lead underwriter or brokerage firm. The IPO will start at a specific price which is usually reserved for the premier clients of the brokerage firm. These clients then have the right to start selling those shares to the general public so that we can buy and sell those shares as well.

The stock market uses measuring tools to determine how well the market is doing. The most well-known tool that the market has is called the Dow Jones Average, which is a widely quoted financial index in the world. On average, the Dow Jones consists of 15-30 companies that broadly define the U.S. economy that generates the measuring stick for how that industry is doing. There are four types of Dow Jones Averages: The Industrial Average (DJIA) consists of 30 stocks that represent areas of public interest. Companies on the DJIA include General Electric, Home Depot, and IBM. The Transportation Average consists of 20 transportation stocks that represent the transportation market. Companies on this list include American Airlines, Avis Budget Group Inc., and Norfolk Southern. The Utility Average (DJUA) is made up of 15 utility stocks, including Edison International, American Electric Power Company Inc., and Duke Energy. Finally, the Composite Average is made up of a combination of the other three averages, 57 of the companies traded on the NYSE, 8 traded on the NASDAQ.

These averages determine whether the stock market is in a bull market or a bear market. A bull market describes the stock market being on the rise, and the bear market describes the stock market being on the decline. The trend of the market over the years has been in between a secular long-term down market; there is a burst of a bull market for a few short months. However, from 1982 to 2000, we entered the opposite of a secular bull market with a few short months of a bear market. This included the bear market of 1987, where the market lost 22% in one day.

To give you a sense of where the Dow Jones lies, here is a quick historical mark of the DJIA. In 1966, the DJIA was at a mere 874. Sixteen years later, in 1982, the DJIA was up to a whopping 875. In the previous paragraph, I mentioned the rare secular bull market that started in 1982. In ten years of that bull market, the DJIA started its skyrocket up to 2000. By the year 2000, the DJIA towered over 11,700. In 2018, the DJIA climbed up to 25,628, which is a one-year change of 13.68%, just short of the DJIA all-time high since its first closing of 62.76 in the year 1885.

In addition to the DJIA, there are other benchmarks that are used to measure the stock market climate. The Standard and Poor's 500 is an American stock index that differs from the DJIA because of its diverse constituency of 500 stocks and its weighting methodology, which makes it one of the best representations of the US stock market. The Wilshire 5000 Total Market Index is the broadest index for the US equity market as it measures the performance of all headquartered equity securities. The Wilshire now actually consists of over 6,300 stocks for its consideration. All these indexes are particularly important in evaluating and monitoring the progress of our own portfolios during these periods.

Now, how do actual trades on the stock market work? In the movie, Trading Places, starring Eddie Murphy and Dan Aykroyd, there was a scene where they were trading on the floor with a bunch of pieces of paper in their hand as they bought and sold stocks at the perfect moment based on some inside reports they had stolen concerning the production of orange juice. In keeping that visual, purchasing stock is no more than receiving a stock certificate made of paper for an invested price. This piece of paper represents ownership in the company. By deciding to sell the stock certificate, the trade process takes place on Wall

Street. A broker will advertise on the exchange that your stock is for sale. There is always someone on the stock exchange willing to buy. There are four ways to list or purchase stock on the exchange. The first is at market order. This means that as soon as the stock is listed for purchase, it is sold at the price the market is currently asking for it. There are no delays as someone is ready to purchase it, as said before. The second is bid & ask prices. These are the highest and the lowest offers that will be taken in selling the stock giving a range for the stock to be sold.

The third is the Limit order, and the stop sells limit order. As their names state, there is a limit on the price at which the order will execute. In a stop-limit order, there are two prices specified- the stop price that will convert the order to a sell order and the limit price. Stop-limit orders are used when the investor does not want to sell if the price of the stock or other security falls below the limit and is willing to wait for the price to rise back to the limit price. Let's say that Jeff has a stock that never drops to the stop-loss price, but it continues to rise and eventually reaches $75 a share. He cancels his stop-loss order at $63 and puts in a stop-limit order at $70 with a limit of $67. If the stock price falls below $70, then the order becomes a live sell-limit order. If the stock price falls below $67 before Frank's order is filled, then the order will remain unfilled until the price climbs back to $67.

The fourth is the stop-loss order. The stop-loss order protects long positions by triggering a market sell order if the price falls below a certain level. The philosophy behind this is if the price falls this far down, it may continue to fall much further, so the loss is capped by selling at that price. So, if Jeff owns 1,000 shares of stock, he purchased the stock at $70 a share, and it has risen to $85 on rumors of a potential buyout. He wants to lock in a gain of at least $11 per share, so he places a sell-stop order at $81. If the stock drops back below this price, the order will become a market order and get filled at the current market price, which may be more (or more likely less) than the stop-loss price of $81. In this case, Jeff might get $81 for 500 shares and $80.50 for the rest. But he will get to keep most of his gain.

For the sake of this quick guide, we have covered the essence of the stock market and the gist of how it operates so that we are able to make the best of our investment. The last thing we need to cover is the basic predictors of stock performance. These are measures that experienced investors use to determine if a stock is worth consideration and whether it is time for it to be bought, sold, or held onto. The first predictor of stock performance is the Price-Earnings Ratio referred to as the P/E. This, in summary, is the price of the stock divided by the company's earnings per share. For a stock to be considered a great bargain, the earnings per share should parallel close to the price of the stock. In other words, the lower the P/E, the more stable the stock and the better the bargain for a buy and for the price of the stock to move up. As the P/E grows higher, the stock starts to become more unstable and become riskier. As a rule of thumb, it is more encouraging to see the P/E ratio at 20 or less. If the P/E starts to rise above 20, the risk of the stock needs to be assessed with other predictors.

The next predictor is the book value. The book value is a measure of the worth of the company's assets, including the estate of the company, its equipment, patents, inventory, cash, etc., minus the company's liabilities, including the shareholder's equity and the accumulated depreciation. Book Value, in accordance with the accounting value of a company, has two main uses: 1) It can indicate whether a stock is overpriced or underpriced at its current market value. 2) It presents the total value of the company's assets that, in theory, would be received by the stockholders if there was legal precedence to liquidate the company.

The third predictor of stock performance is dividends. Dividends are the distributions of a company's earnings to shareholders paid out every quarter along with the company quarterly reports. Dividends indicate that the stock is of a company that is a larger, established one in a sector or industry such as pharmaceuticals, healthcare, oil & gas, and utilities. These companies, solid and steady, are not trying to sustain higher-than-average growth and expansion. It can also signal if a company is in trouble if the dividend is reduced or eliminated, as well as if there is an unexpected increase in the dividend rate being a sign that the company is on the rise. This directly correlates with the next predictor, which is the yield. Yield is simply the return that is being received by the shareholders in the form of dividends on the shares of stocks owned expressed in percentages. Both predictors give vital information that shows the next predictor, which is volatility. Volatility is the fluctuation of the stock prices relative to the overall stock market, whether it is rising or falling. Volatility is tracked with a measurement known as the beta. If beta is greater than 1, that represents the stock is very volatile; if the beta is less than 1, then the stock is less volatile than the overall market. It refers to the amount of uncertainty or risk about the size of changes in a security's value. A higher volatility means the stock price and value can potentially spread over a large range and can change dramatically over a short period in either direction. The volatility index is used to maintain the barometer on the equity market and offers investors a means to manage risk and better diversify their portfolio.

The last two predictors directly involve the management output of the company. Debt/Equity (D/E) ratio is commonly used to determine the company's financial leverage in the market. This ratio is calculated by dividing the company's liabilities by its stockholder's equity. It indicates how much debt a company is using to finance its assets regarding value represented in the shareholder's equity. For example, consider a company that has a total shareholder equity value of $220,000 and has $733,000 in liabilities. That means its D/E ratio is 3.3318 ($733,000/ $220,000), or 333.18%, indicating that the company has been taking on an extreme amount of debt and thus is extremely risky. On the other hand, if the company has a shareholder value of $733,000 and $220,000 in liabilities, the company's D/E ratio is 0.3001 ($220,000/ $733,000), or 30.01%, indicating the company has taken on relatively little debt and thus has low risk. The last predictor of stock performance is revenues. Revenues are the amount of money that a corporation takes in from sales of its products and services each year. It is considered the "gross income" from which operational costs are subtracted to determine the net income. It is also referred to as sales and is used in calculating the price-to-sales ratio, which is the alternative to the previously mentioned price-to-earnings ratio where revenue is used instead of earnings. When public companies report quarterly earnings, the two amounts that receive focused attention are revenue and earnings per share, with earnings equating to net income.

This is the information needed to get started in investing in the stock market of our own volition. It is also the beginning of becoming an informed investor. Unfortunately, the days of working for a company for 30 years, then retiring with a sizable pension are over.

Control of retirement has been handed over to the individuals, so our purpose is to make sure you have the skills and tools as well as a blueprint for a successful investment strategy. The next chapter will take the information that we have discussed in the previous two chapters and define that blueprint as given by one of the most successful investors in the United States.

Chapter 12:

The Four Economic Seasons and The All Seasons Portfolio

Now it is time to reveal the blueprint that, in my opinion, through my research, will give you the best chance of achieving the most with your investments. I have been a big fan of Tony Robbins ever since he came out with his Unlimited Power Series on cassette tape over 20 years ago. In his book, Money: Master the Game: 7 Simple Steps to Financial Freedom, he talks about a hedge fund owner named Ray Dalio who came up with a formula he calls The All Seasons Portfolio. Although you may have never heard of Ray Dalio, recognize that his name is amid major conversations in high places in the financial world. Two things you should know about him: 1) Dalio runs the world's largest hedge fund that consisted of nearly $160 billion dollars under its watch (most large hedge funds contain around $15 billion). 2) Dalio's financial genius is the reason why McDonald's Chicken McNuggets exists today. His funds have had extraordinary returns of nearly 10% annually for over 40 years (1974 thru 2013), and there were only six losses during those 40 years, with the average loss being only -1.47%! The worst loss was only -3.93%. In looking for a formula of a portfolio that considers the possible seasons of the market, your age, your risk tolerance, and your investment goals, this one was the seller for me. So, I will share the overall portfolio with you. If you desire more information on both the portfolio and its founder, please go buy a copy of Tony Robbins' book.

For the All Seasons Portfolio to make complete sense to you, I would first like to go over the seasons that have the tendency to move and influence the price of assets. Every investment has an ideal environment in which it was designed to flourish. It just so happens that there are four economic seasons that you must be aware of that create four different possible environments that affect whether investments will go up or down. The Four Seasons that move the price of assets are: 1) Inflation, 2) Deflation, 3) Rising Economic Growth, and 4) Declining Economic Growth. If you look at Table #4, there are two factors that determine the behavior of the market: Inflation and Economic Growth. In any season, these two factors will either rise or fall. Thus, we have the Four Seasons. If the market is showing a rise in the prices of goods sold, then the market is yielding higher than expected inflation. If the market is showing prices of goods sold falling, then the market is yielding lower than expected inflation. Both of those seasons are the results of economic inflation. The next two seasons are affected directly by economic growth.

Table #4: Four Seasons That Move The Price of Assets

1) Inflation
2) Deflation
3) Rising Economic Growth
4) Declining Economic Growth

	Growth	*Inflation*
Rising	Higher than expected Economic Growth	Higher than Expected Inflation
Falling	Lower than Expected Economic Growth	Lower than Expected Inflation

(Robbins, MONEY, pp. 390)

If the market is in a Rising Economic Growth mode, then the market is yielding higher than expected economic growth. If the market is in a Declining Economic Growth mode, then the market is yielding lower than expected economic growth. What does this all mean? Just like the four climate seasons of summer, fall, winter, and spring, each economic season has its own characteristics, and our overall investments must consider for each season. The only difference is that there is no apparent order of which economic season will come next. There are good and bad environments for all the asset classes. We must expect that sooner or later, one of those asset classes will have a ruinous environment at some point in our lifetime. Our goal is to construct a portfolio that will do well in the year 2027, even though we do not know how the seasons will play out in the world and what it will look like in 2027. If we can learn to spread an equal amount of risk in all four portfolios, we can keep ourselves from being exposed to any environment.

If we look at Table #5, it lays out which seasons the different forms of investments thrive in best. If economic growth is rising, the best investment venues to have are: Stocks, Corporate Bonds, Commodities, Gold. In fact, Commodities and Gold thrive best when either factor is RISING! Stocks, on the other hand, are at their best when either economic growth is rising OR when inflation is falling. There are two seasons for all the above mentioned except Corporate Bonds.

Table #5: Investment Venues Relative to the Economic Season

	Growth	***Inflation***
Rising	Stocks, Commodities, Corporate Bonds, Gold	Commodities, Gold, Inflation Linked Bonds (TIPS)
Falling	Treasury Bonds, Inflation Linked Bonds (TIPS)	Treasury Bonds, Stocks

(Robbins, MONEY, pp. 390)

Corporate Bonds only thrive when economic growth is rising; they do not do well when the market is being affected by inflation either way. So, there goes the theory of a balanced portfolio consisting of 50% stocks and 50% bonds. Yes, your portfolio has an even number of stocks and bonds this way, but your risk and coverage in the Four Seasons are unbalanced. In addition, always keep in mind that stocks are 3 times more volatile than bonds!

What is the last element that we can use that will make our portfolio profitable when inflation starts to act up? Well, leave it to Ray Dalio to have created the legal structure for Treasury Inflation Protected Securities (TIPS) in 1997. TIPS thrives best when inflation is on the rise and when economic growth is on the decline. TIPS protects us against spikes in inflation. (Table #5) shows that if we were to buy $10,000 worth of TIPS at 1.5% interest and the Consumer Price Index doesn't change in six months, the "Par Value" remains the same, and we would get a $150 interest payment. The beauty of TIPS is if the cost of living goes up 2%, our bond is now worth $10,200, and the semiannual payment is now $153. By owning a lot of TIPS in our structured portfolio and there is a lot of inflation, our TIPS money will start to add up!

Table #6: Raymond James TIPS Chart

Raymond James TIPS Chart

Years	Coupon	Per Value	Period of Inflation	Change in CPI	Adjusted Principal	Interest Payment
1	1.5%	$1,000	Inflationary	+2%	$1,020	$15.30
2	1.5%	$1,020	Deflationary	-1%	$1,010	$15.15
3	1.5%	$1,010	Inflationary	+3%	$1,040	$15.60
4	1.5%	$1,040	Inflationary	+2%	$1,060	$15.90
5	1.5%	$1,060	Inflationary	+1%	$1,070	$16.05

(Robbins, MONEY, pp. 319)

Finally, there are Treasury Bonds that thrive best when either economic growth or inflation is falling.

Now the question from this All Seasons information is, "can we construct a properly balanced portfolio to handle All Seasons of the economy?" Well, I am glad that Tony Robbins was friends enough with Ray Dalio, who was gracious enough to give out his winning portfolio distribution that got his great returns over a 40-year period. In Chart #18, it should be noted how the All Seasons portfolio performed against the worst years that the S&P market has dropped since 1937 and the comparison between the two.

Chart #20: Standards and Poor's vs. All Seasons Worst Drops

S&P vs. All Seasons Worst Drops

Year	S&P	All Seasons
1937	-35.03%	-9.00%
1941	-11.59%	-1.69%
1973	-14.69%	3.67%
1974	-26.47%	-1.16%
2001	-11.89%	-1.91%
2002	-22.10%	7.87%
2008	-37.00%	-3.93%

(Robbins, MONEY, pp. 397-398)

Now Ray's "All Weather" strategy has a lot more complex and sophisticated investment tactics attached to it. This All Seasons portfolio has the same core principles and the specific percentages designed directly by Ray and no one else.

Chart #21: Standard and Poor vs. All Season Comparison

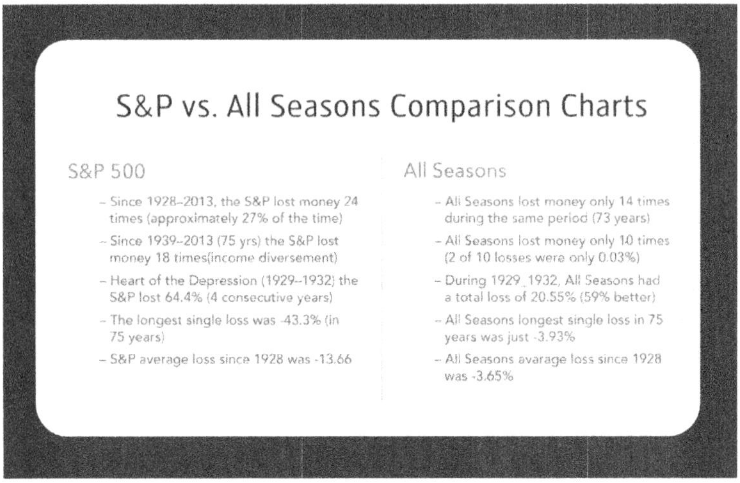

(Robbins, MONEY, pp. 396-397)

We can see how the portfolio is distributed between economic growth (grow) and inflation (flat).

1) Stocks (up grow; down flat) Index Funds --- 30%
2) Long Term US Bonds (down grow; down flat) --- 20%
3) Long Term US TIPS (down grow; up flat) --- 20%
4) Intermediate US Bonds (down grow; down flat) -- 15%
5) Gold (up grow; up flat) --- 07.5%
6) Commodities (up grow; up flat) --- 07.5%

Even though history does not guarantee future performance, it is the most comfortable and confident portfolio I have ever seen in my 22 years of investing. So, here it goes.

Chart #22: Four Season Diversified Portfolio

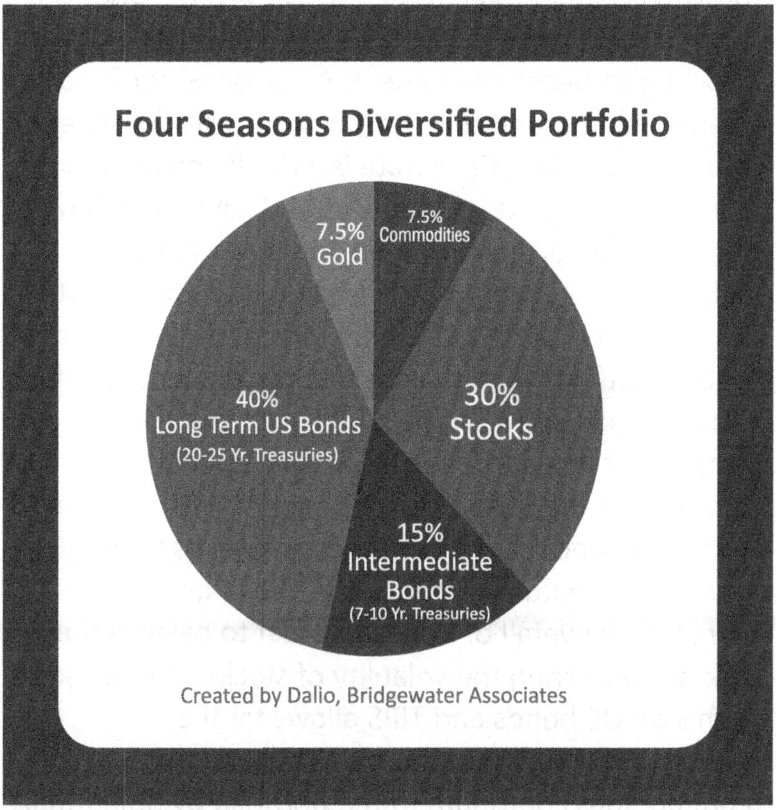

(Robbins, MONEY, pp. 393-394)

<u>Notes:</u>

Author- Ray Dalio, CEO, Bridgewater Associates
The portfolio must be rebalanced at least annually, if not every 6 months. When one segment does

well, sell a portion and reallocate back to the original allocation. If done properly, it can increase tax efficiency.

It is important to note that Corporate Bonds behave in the same manner that stocks do when the economic growth is higher than expected. However, it does not work the same way as stocks do in a deflation market. Stocks give better coverage in All Seasons portfolio than would Corporate Bonds; however, stocks are also more volatile than Corporate Bonds. If you are more conservative about your returns and have more time for investments to grow, then you may want to substitute 5% of your stock investment for corporate bonds. Now, as we analyze the percentage makeup of the portfolio, it may seem that our percentage of stock ownership would be a little low. But the purpose of this portfolio is to balance out the risk between all the possible economic seasons. Keep in mind that stocks are three times as risky as bonds just due to their nature. Thus, comes the larger percentage overall of bonds in order to balance the risk by countering the volatility of stocks. The longer terms on US bonds and TIPS allows for the opportunity for higher returns. The gold and commodities contribute to the portfolio by doing well when inflation accelerates even though they are also highly volatile. As we experienced in 2008, there are environments that accelerated inflation can have a toll on both stocks and bonds. The small percentage of gold and commodities helps to counter this.

One of the most important factors about the All Seasons portfolio is that it helps us balance our investment risk as opposed to dollar amounts. It is very important to rebalance the portfolio at least once or twice a year. Since stocks are three times riskier than bonds, if the stocks end up having a great year, the gains due to the stock will cause the percentages to shift and cause the portfolio to come out of balance. Whereas, when the year started, your stocks consisted of 30% of the portfolio, after the gains have been added, stocks may now consist of 42% of the portfolio. In order to keep the portfolio balanced, it becomes necessary that the excess 12% of stocks be sold and redistributed so that the portfolio maintains the risk-balanced percentages. If you are not comfortable in redistributing the gains yourself, this is where having a good independent fiduciary can help in managing your portfolio. Reallocating done properly will increase your tax efficiency.

Chart #23: Yale University Alternative Portfolio

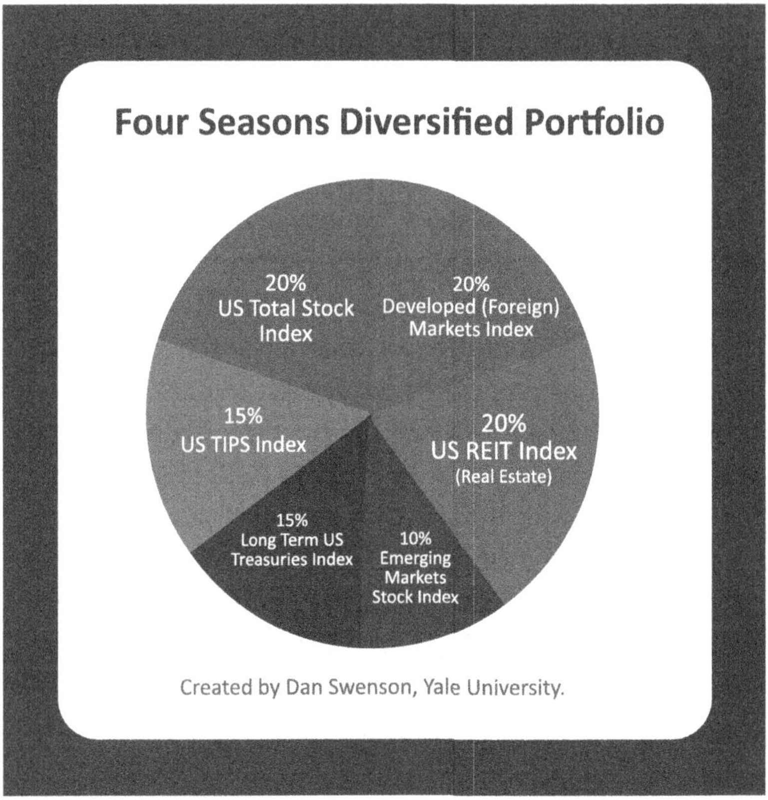

(Robbins, MONEY, pp. 407-408)

Of course, this is not the only portfolio plan that will help you to balance your investment risk. You may be interested in investing in Real Estate Investment Trusts Indexes or emerging and/or foreign index markets, as shown in Chart #22. But it is a great simplified plan that will help you get started if this is your first time investing. My recommendation would be to keep investing in index funds that have treasury bonds first, then start to add stocks ending up with gold and commodities, and your investment amount grows. The more you invest, the greater your financial empowerment becomes, and the more astute you will become in matching your goals with your portfolio.

Epilogue:

It's Not About Money, But the Fluid Flow of Finances: The Final Piece to the Puzzle

The movie "Passengers," starring Chris Pratt and Jennifer Lawrence, was about a colony of people who were on a spaceship heading to a new planet that took 120 years of space travel to get there from the earth. The spaceship runs into a meteor storm, and its impact causes the ship's computer frame to malfunction, waking up one of the passengers (Chris Pratt) out of hibernation 90 years before he was supposed to wake up. It demonstrated the struggle of adapting to a life where you are all alone in a foreign place, taking a journey to a destination of the unknown. The ship was designed in the form of a three-dimensional helix shape spinning along its axis to where from behind, it looked like a wheel turning in space. I make mention of this movie because your life has now the opportunity to shift out of hibernation. You can start a new financial destination. Will you? What will you do now that you have been made aware of the new possibilities with the current financial information?

This money management lesson just scratched the surface to make you aware. Will you change your course and become a student of being a financial steward? Will you become disciplined and live your life with the new skills and tools that you have been given? Or will you continue to choke on your old spending habits and lack of money discipline being broke for the rest of your days on this earth? Your new discipline is your awakening out of hibernation, and the spaceship represents your newly found financial resources that are taking you on a new course to a new destination.

It is not about the money. There are a lot of people who make this assumption. It is about the fluid flow of your finances. The fluid flow of your finances is all about the value you bring to others. The more value that you can bring to other people, the more fluid flow your finances will bring you. Investing is not contrary to bringing value to others. The discipline of investing allows more opportunity to give to others which in turn brings in more money to invest. So instead of asking, "How can I be wealthier?", the question to ask is, "How can I be more valuable?" There is no shame in pursuing the almighty dollar, but it should be in the context of fulfilling the financial fluid flow and its value. Our spiritual wealth and financial wealth must go hand in hand to maintain the fluid financial flow.

This quick guide to money management would not be complete if I did not give references to other works that are must-reads to continue your course work in becoming a financial steward. A lot of the information in this quick guide was referenced to some degree from the following works, which I consider must-reads:

1) Tony Robbins' New York Times Best Seller, Money- Master The Game: 7 Simple Steps to Financial Freedom. If you need more details regarding the four economic seasons and the investment formula, this is a must reference.

2) Dennis Kimbro's The Wealth Choice: Success Secrets of Black Millionaires. It is best to follow by example of people who have already done it. As you start your journey on financial stewardship, this is the read that will help you take your beginning steps.

3) T. Harv Eker's Secrets of the Millionaire Mind: Mastering the Inner Game of Wealth. His motto is you have to "Think Rich to Get Rich!" Find out what your "money blueprint" really is so that you can convert what's holding you back from becoming successful in bringing your success into reality.

4) Hill Harper's The Wealth Cure: Putting Money In Its Place. Sometimes we place money way above where it is supposed to reside. Harper goes through scenarios where he has misappropriated money that, in starting out on this new journey, gives us something to

think about and put money in its proper perspective.

5) Chris Hogan's Retire Inspired: It's Not an Age, It's a Financial Number. Whenever we reference the word retirement, it is great to be reminded that the earlier we start creating our nest egg, the better off we will be when we enter our golden years. So, we must focus on our retirement from day one of earning a paycheck, if not before.

The life of an investor is the road less traveled, but the road most rewarding. Make no mistake, this journey can be a lonely one, but you will be happy with where the destination leads you.

References

Cooper, B. (2018). *Eloquent rage: A black feminist discovers her superpower.* St. Martin's Press.

Cooper, B. (2018). Patriarchy is a Structural Problem. In *Eloquent rage: A black feminist discovers her superpower* (pp. 80-85). St. Martin's Press.

Eker, T. H. (2005). *Secrets of the millionaire mind: Mastering the inner game of wealth.* Toronto, Ontario, Canada: HarperCollins.

Eker, T. H. (2005). Hoarders, Spenders, Avoiders, Money Monks. In *Secrets of the millionaire mind: Mastering the inner game of wealth* (pp. 40-45). Toronto, Ontario, Canada: HarperCollins.

Eker, T. H. (2005). Wealth File #1- "I will not blame, complain, or justify my situation.". In *Secrets of the millionaire mind: Mastering the inner game of wealth* (pp. 54-62). Toronto, Ontario, Canada: HarperCollins.

Eker, T. H. (2005). Wealth File #3- "Rich people are committed to being rich, Poor people want to be rich". In *Secrets of the millionaire mind: Mastering the inner game of wealth* (pp. 65-68). Toronto, Ontario, Canada: HarperCollins.

Eker, T. H. (2005). Wealth File #5- "Rich People focus on Opportunities, Poor people focus on Obstacles". In *Secrets of the millionaire mind: Mastering the inner game of wealth* (pp. 78-79). Toronto, Ontario, Canada: HarperCollins.

Eker, T. H. (2005). Wealth File #9- “Rich are bigger than their Problems, Poor are smaller than their problems”. In *Secrets of the millionaire mind: Mastering the inner game of wealth* (pp. 106-108). Toronto, Ontario, Canada: HarperCollins.

Eker, T. H. (2005). Wealth File #16- “Rich People Act In Spite of Fear, Poor People Let Fear Stop Them”. In *Secrets of the millionaire mind: Mastering the inner game of wealth* (pp. 166-167). Toronto, Ontario, Canada: HarperCollins.

Eker, T. H. (2005). Wealth File #17- “Rich People Constantly Learn and Grow, Poor People Think They Already Know”. In *Secrets of the millionaire mind: Mastering the inner game of wealth* (pp. 179-184). Toronto, Ontario, Canada: HarperCollins.

Kimbro, D. P. (2014). *The wealth choice: Success secrets of black millionaires*. Basingstoke: Palgrave Macmillan.

Kimbro, D. P. (2014). Concept: The Calculus of Compensation. In *The wealth choice: Success secrets of black millionaires* (pp. 91-92). Basingstoke: Palgrave Macmillan.

Kimbro, D. P. (2014). Table- Nine Drivers of Wealth. In *The wealth choice: Success secrets of black millionaires* (pp. 92). Basingstoke: Palgrave Macmillan.

Kimbro, D. P. (2014). Senator Daniel Patrick Moynihan. In *The wealth choice: Success secrets of black millionaires* (pp. 93). Basingstoke: Palgrave Macmillan.

Kimbro, D. P. (2014). Driver #4- Act Rich/ Act Poor. In *The wealth choice: Success secrets of black millionaires* (pp. 96-97). Basingstoke: Palgrave Macmillan.

Eker, T. H. (2014). How Millionaires Use The Power of Faith and Belief. In 1245728984 923456084 D. P. Kimbro (Author), *The wealth choice: Success secrets of black millionaires* (p. 137). Basingstoke: Palgrave Macmillan.

Kimbro, D. P. (2014). Definition of Capital (Latin). In *The wealth choice: Success secrets of black millionaires* (pp.155). Basingstoke: Palgrave Macmillan.

Kimbro, D. P. (2014). Much is Required. In *The wealth choice: Success secrets of black millionaires* (pp. 210-211). Basingstoke: Palgrave Macmillan.

Kimbro, D. P. (2014). New Rules of Money: Fire Your Boss. In *The wealth choice: Success secrets of black millionaires* (pp. 241-244). Basingstoke: Palgrave Macmillan.

Kimbro, D. P. (2014). Five Wealth Building Strategies Of The Black Financial Elite. In *The wealth choice: Success secrets of black millionaires* (pp. 261-265). Basingstoke: Palgrave Macmillan.

Robbins, T. (2016). *Money master the game 7 simple steps to financial freedom*. London: Simon & Schuster.

Robbins, T. (2016). Doubling the Dollar a Day vs w/ 33% Tax. In *Money master the game 7 simple steps to financial freedom* (pp. 35-36). London: Simon & Schuster.

Robbins, T. (2016). Chart- Points of Maximum Financial Risk and Opportunity. In *Money master the game 7 simple steps to financial freedom* (pp. 96). London: Simon & Schuster.

Robbins, T. (2016). Chart- Impact of Fees. In *Money master the game 7 simple steps to financial freedom* (pp. 107). London: Simon & Schuster.

Robbins, T. (2016). Chart- Mutual Fund True Cost. In *Money master the game 7 simple steps to financial freedom* (pp. 112). London: Simon & Schuster.

Robbins, T. (2016). Table- Broker vs Fiduciary. In *Money master the game 7 simple steps to financial freedom* (pp. 139). London: Simon & Schuster.

Robbins, T. (2016). Definition of Financial Security. In *Money master the game 7 simple steps to financial freedom* (pp. 214-219). London: Simon & Schuster.

Robbins, T. (2016). Chart- Interest Fees Over Time. In *Money master the game 7 simple steps to financial freedom* (pp. 252). London: Simon & Schuster.

Robbins, T. (2016). Chart- The Golden Egg. In *Money master the game 7 simple steps to financial freedom* (pp. 277). London: Simon & Schuster.

Robbins, T. (2016). Chart- Number of Years to Double Your Investment Based on Rate of Return. In *Money master the game 7 simple steps to financial freedom* (pp. 286). London: Simon & Schuster.

Robbins, T. (2016). Table: Raymond James TIPS Chart. In *Money master the game 7 simple steps to financial freedom* (pp. 318-319). London: Simon & Schuster.

Robbins, T. (2016). What Are You Willing To Risk Game Show. In *Money master the game 7 simple steps to financial freedom* (pp. 334). London: Simon & Schuster.

Robbins, T. (2016). The Great Test. In *Money master the game 7 simple steps to financial freedom* (pp. 358-359). London: Simon & Schuster.

Robbins, T. (2016). Chart- Four Things That Move the Price of Assets. In *Money master the game 7 simple steps to financial freedom* (pp. 388). London: Simon & Schuster.

Robbins, T. (2016). Give Me The Numbers. In *Money master the game 7 simple steps to financial freedom* (pp. 392-393). London: Simon & Schuster.

Robbins, T. (2016). S&P 500 vs All Seasons Since 1928. In *Money master the game 7 simple steps to financial freedom* (pp. 397). London: Simon & Schuster.

Robbins, T. (2016). David Swenson "Other Ways to Skin a Cat". In *Money master the game 7 simple steps to financial freedom* (pp. 407). London: Simon & Schuster.

Robbins, T. (2016). Flip-Flop Gains, John vs Susan. In *Money master the game 7 simple steps to financial freedom* (pp. 419-422). London: Simon & Schuster.

Made in United States
North Haven, CT
10 November 2026

22088890R00114